HISTORIC PHOTOS OF
THE CHINESE IN
CALIFORNIA

TEXT AND CAPTIONS BY
HANNAH CLAYBORN

TURNER
PUBLISHING COMPANY

The flag of the new Chinese Republic flew over the Chinese village at the Panama Pacific International Exposition in 1915, and the ancient golden dragon, Gum Lung, so familiar to San Franciscans, was banished in the new revolutionary spirit. Inside the pavilions visitors viewed magnificent carvings, vases, lacquered furniture, and a priceless private collection of paintings on silk, the finest of its kind in the world.

HISTORIC PHOTOS OF
THE CHINESE IN
CALIFORNIA

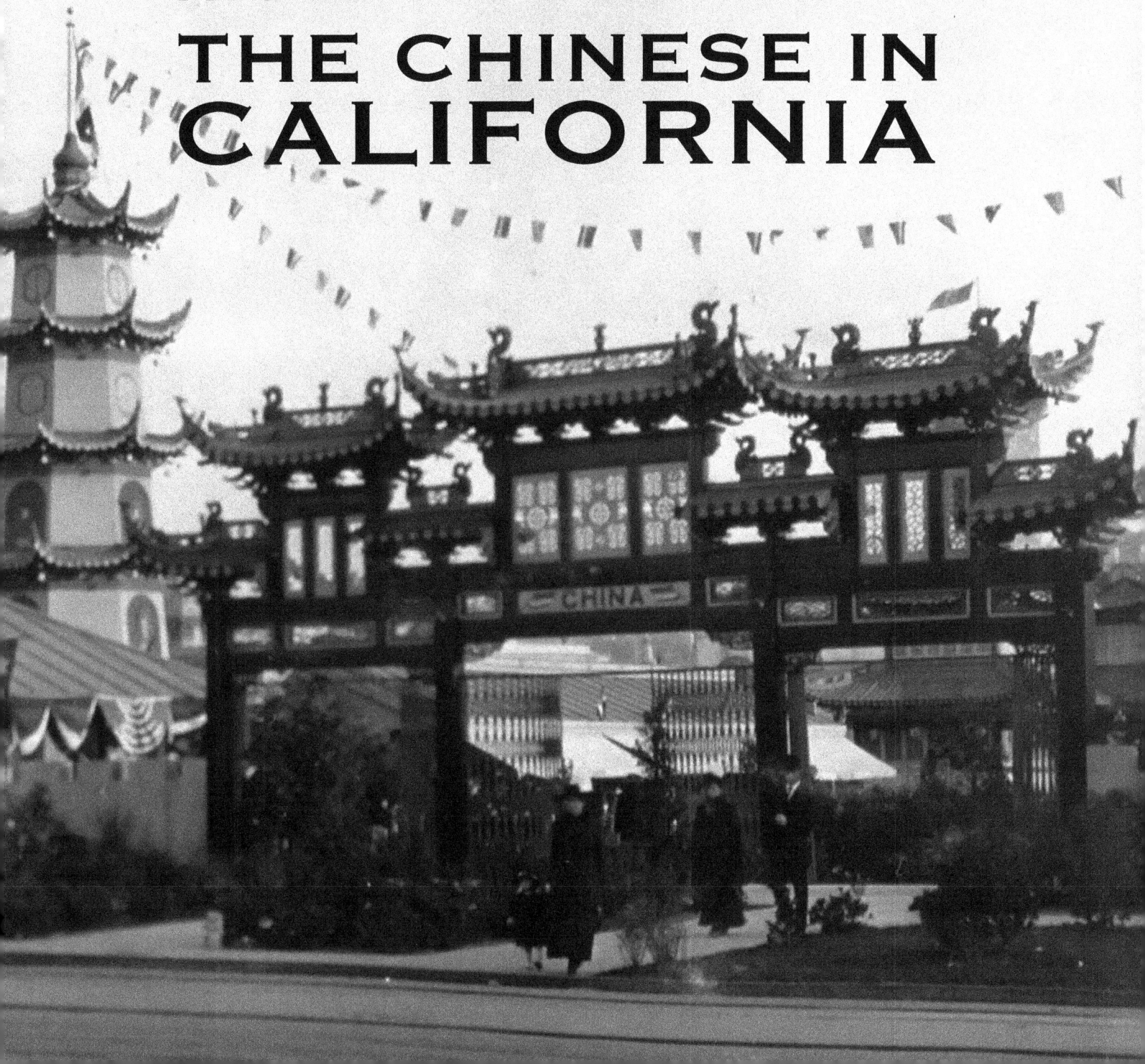

Turner Publishing Company
www.turnerpublishing.com

Historic Photos of the Chinese in California

Copyright © 2009 Turner Publishing Company

Library of Congress Control Number: 2008941040

ISBN-13: 978-1-59652-519-1

Printed in the United States of America

ISBN 978-1-68442-076-6 (hc)

CONTENTS

Although this photo is labeled as showing a Chinese store in a fishing village near Monterey, ca. 1900, the gods mounted in front of the building may indicate a joss house. J. R. Fitch described a Chinese fishing village at Monterey in 1888: "The long poles that adorn the fronts of most of the houses, the crazy balconies built out over the water, the fluttering rags that hang from clothes-lines, the queer boats, with their lateen-sails, [and] the children with their red and yellow garments . . . When viewed from the water, it is said . . . to bear a striking resemblance to the native villages that line the Yangtse and other great rivers of the Flowery Kingdom." [From: *Picturesque California,* John Muir, editor, 1888]

Acknowledgments

This volume, *Historic Photos of the Chinese in California,* is the result of the cooperation and efforts of many individuals, organizations, and corporations. It is with great thanks that we acknowledge the valuable contribution of the following for their generous support:

The Bancroft Library, University of California, Berkeley

Butte County Pioneer Memorial Museum, Oroville, California

The California History Room, California State Library, Sacramento, California

Kings County Library

Library of Congress

Oroville Chinese Temple & Museum, Oroville, California

San Francisco History Center, San Francisco Public Library

We would also like to thank the following individuals for valuable contributions and assistance in making this work possible:

Gloria S. Brown

Jenny Chen-Yu Lin

Ed Clausen

Patricia Clayborn

David Dewey

Cindy Huynh Howland

William Wong

May Lum Young

This book is dedicated to John, Cleone, and Cyrene

With the exception of touching up imperfections that have accrued over time and cropping where necessary, no other changes have been made. The focus and clarity of many images is limited by the technology and the ability of the photographer at the time they were taken.

PREFACE

In the years between the discovery of gold in 1848 and the enforcement of the Chinese Exclusion Act of 1882, more than 75,000 Chinese nationals made their way to California. Yet finding historical documentation of this first generation of Chinese immigrants can be a frustrating endeavor. In the 1970s, evidence of a Chinese community emerged during my research into the history of Bloomfield, a "ghost town" in rural Sonoma County that had blossomed in stagecoach days, only to wither when bypassed by the railroad. Although not a word about the Chinese in Bloomfield appeared in print, Bloomfield's oldest residents, recounting their own childhood memories and tales told by their parents, described the Chinese workers who lived by the hundreds in shacks or the back rooms and basements of commercial buildings along a Bloomfield street that old-timers, without a hint of disrespect, still called "Pigtail Alley."

Chinese immigrants built Bloomfield's early wells and reservoirs and for three decades formed the main labor force that enriched pioneer landowners and farmers. But nineteenth-century county historians had intentionally ignored the Chinese, and their published works formed the foundation for later researchers. Bloomfield's history is neither unique nor uncommon.

Like argonauts from other nations who quit the California gold fields, the Chinese originally dispersed throughout the state wherever there were jobs or a living to be made. Laws prohibited them from owning land, and so they gravitated largely to agricultural areas and reclamation or construction projects. But increasingly in the decades following the gold rush, the Chinese became targets for hostility that reached levels faced by no other immigrant group.

Informants in Bloomfield also remembered why the Chinese left their town. According to town lore, some residents poisoned the drinking wells of the Chinese workers, killing 17 before driving all of them out of town one terrible night in the 1880s. Most Bloomfield Chinese probably fled to urban centers like San Francisco's Chinatown, where they would be joined by thousands of their countrymen. Those few who took refuge in neighboring Sonoma County towns were said to have declaimed starkly in reference to Bloomfield, "We walk around that hill," refusing even to utter its name. It is my guess that the great majority of the acts of violence and racism rained upon the Chinese during the economic depression that began in the 1870s went largely unrecorded, and remain so.

Because so little about the lives, achievements, and suffering of the first generation of Chinese in California was recorded, historic photographs are an invaluable documentation of their enduring presence. In this volume, images have been gathered from some of the most notable collections in the state, including the works of famous photographers and images that have never been published. Each is a small window between past and present. Together they offer a perspective of the journey of many Chinese Americans living in California today.

Although San Francisco's Chinatown was the undisputed capital of the Chinese in America from the very earliest years of the gold rush, there were many other Chinatowns. For example, thousands of Chinese settled in and around Oroville, where the Feather River flows out into the Central Valley. They mined and worked on the Central Pacific Railroad until a major flood forced them to relocate in 1907. The Central Pacific Railroad built the town of Hanford in the San Joaquin Valley in 1877, and hundreds of Chinese railroad workers stayed on there, eventually supporting a Taoist Temple, a Chinese Center of Knowledge, and a block of commercial buildings that boasted a famous herbalist.

A Chinatown developed across the bay from San Francisco in Oakland. With more open land, better weather, and work available on railroads and farms, Oakland's Chinatown already had a sizeable population when the 1906 earthquake and fire forced many refugees from San Francisco to relocate there. Coastal fishing villages sprang up in and around Monterey, San Luis Obispo, and San Diego. Chinatown in Los Angeles had its own unique character. First housed in crumbling adobes on Calle de los Negros (Street of the Dark Hued Ones), Chinese businesses later surrounded three sides of El Pueblo Plaza. At its height in 1900, it had 200 buildings spread over about 15 streets and alleys, including an opera house, three temples, and a telephone exchange.

Yet photographers, both amateur and professional, were drawn overwhelmingly to San Francisco's "gilded ghetto." Obvious dangers and lack of work in other parts of California had swollen Chinatown's mostly male population to about 22,000 by 1885, and because of local residential restrictions, they were all living in just 12 square blocks. The novelty of such concentrated cultural intensity, from gorgeous embroidered Imperial garb, to sidewalks filled with live chickens and produce, to the sweet smell of opium smoke, created an irresistible impulse in both tourist and artist to record the scene. And so each of Chinatown's streets and teeming alleyways are captured evolving over time in a small world apart until restrictions were lifted after World War II and the doors of the gilded cage finally opened.

—Hannah Clayborn

News of a gold strike in California spread aboard ships arriving in Guangdong (Canton) Province, China, in 1848. By 1852, the approximate date of this daguerreotype of Euro-American and Chinese miners standing next to a sluice box at the head of Auburn Ravine in Placer County, about 25,000 Chinese had reached Gam Saan, or Gold Mountain, their name for California. Unfairly taxed and unable to own land or file claims, these Chinese men probably labored for wages.

Gam Saan Haak (Guests of Gold Mountain)

Chinese immigrants were a visible current in the tidal wave of humanity that rushed through San Francisco's Golden Gate in the early 1850s. Most came from the Pearl River Delta in Guangdong (Canton) Province. Word of the 1848 gold discovery in California first spread on ships, and the people of Guangdong Province, burdened at home with political corruption, war, and floods, were some of the first to hear of it.

Starting as a trickle of 500 by 1850, there were 25,000 Chinese recorded in California's 1852 census. Their countrymen called them Gam Saan Haak (guests of Gold Mountain). While some foreigners in California could blend with the horde, the Chinese, with their ancient customs and exotic dress, stood out like dark pebbles on a sandy shore. The typical Chinese argonaut was young, single, and uneducated. He intended to return to China with his fortune made.

Most Chinese came through the port of San Francisco, heading for the Sierra foothills, where they encountered many types of discrimination. In the 1850s, local governments made assimilation unlikely by denying most Chinese the right of naturalization. Without citizenship they could neither own land nor file a mining claim. A discriminatory tax leached their profits, and they could not testify against a white man in court. Forced to work abandoned claims or to labor for low wages, the Chinese still managed to find gold and built many of the flumes and roads in the gold fields.

Despite violence and discrimination, the Chinese clung tenaciously to Gold Mountain, taking jobs on road crews, reclaiming marshlands in the Sacramento Delta and Central Valley, digging reservoirs and wells in new towns, and piling stones for property line fences. They opened laundries and became cooks and servants. They joined the ranks of migrant agricultural laborers or sharecropped, growing fine produce even on small plots of land. Chinese fishing villages sprang up along the coast.

Chinese crews competed with other crews, largely Irish, to build the first railroads in California. Working for the Central Pacific, Chinese also built the western portion of the transcontinental railroad, doing the most hazardous tasks involved in laying track over the Sierra Nevada. They suffered and died in blasting accidents or freezing weather, or in acts of violence, recorded and unrecorded, throughout the state. But many more became the ancestors of generations of Chinese Americans, no longer guests of Gold Mountain.

Chinese miners generally wore blue cotton clothing and used simple tools to wash the gold from the rocks and sand of a riverbed, a method known as placer mining. This man is using a cradle, a wooden box with top and front piece missing and a sieve on the bottom side to trap the gold. The photo was probably taken near Jacksonville in Tuolumne County or Mongolian Flat on the American River, ca. 1860.

Some of the first Chinese immigrants to reach the gold fields settled in the rolling foothills of Tuolumne County at Camp Salvado. They were soon driven out by other miners and so resettled at a place known as Chinese Diggings or Chinese Camp. At one time home to an estimated 5,000 Chinese, the settlement reputedly had many urban amenities and several joss houses. Placer mining continued at Chinese Camp until the 1870s. This view dates from about 1865.

While most white miners worked alone or in pairs, Chinese miners often worked in teams. Headed for diggings near Columbia in Tuolumne County in 1866, three of these men wear leather boots and western headgear, while the one on the right, perhaps a more recent arrival, still wears a traditional hat and goes barefoot. Their shovels serve as poles to carry sacks and buckets of supplies. Although their long braids, or queues, are not visible, they may be wound neatly around their heads, the custom for the laboring class.

A man carries tea to the crews blasting the east portal of Tunnel No. 8 of the Central Pacific Railroad, 105 miles from Sacramento near Donner Lake, ca. 1868. Chinese railroad workers reportedly suffered less dysentery than others because they boiled water for tea or cooking. As the number of this tunnel suggests, it was neither the first nor last in the dangerous and brutal job of blasting a roadbed through the high Sierras.

Driven from the mines by discriminatory taxes and violence, Chinese from farming districts gravitated to California's agricultural areas, where they became migrant laborers or sharecropped. By 1870, Chinese made up nearly 25 percent of California's unskilled labor force, but only 10 percent of the state's total population. Ten years later, 99 percent of Chinese in the U.S. lived in the West, nearly three-quarters of them in California. These field workers were photographed about 1880.

A Chinese laborer spreads onion seed to dry on the W. J. Fosgate seed ranch near Santa Clara, ca. 1880. In more remote areas of California in this era, Chinese workers sometimes supplied the majority of farm labor used to support large operations. The vastness of those farms coupled with the paucity of the wages paid to the Chinese workers can be compared to the profitability of the plantations of the pre–Civil War South.

Chinese workers harvest alfalfa hay in the fields of Kern County in 1888. At about this time, hostility and discrimination drove most Chinese workers from rural areas in California. Other groups—some of them immigrants themselves—wanted these jobs at higher wages. Many unrecorded acts of violence against Chinese workers led them to seek refuge in urban centers, where they had some protection in numbers.

Except for his traditional hat, this Chinese ranch hand, photographed by Carleton Watkins in 1888, has adopted western clothing, including what may be Levi Strauss denim jeans, trousers invented in California for rough work at the gold mines. This furnace ran the steam water pump on the McClung Ranch in Kern County.

This group of campers is pictured eating a meal on Mount Shasta in July 1888 in a photograph titled "The Dining Room." Although they enjoyed the romance of rusticity, these middle-class campers nevertheless were unwilling to do without the indispensable services of two Chinese cooks.

This Chinese cook and his young assistant (practicing with a bow and arrow) fed a group known as the "Merry Makers" or the "Merry Tramps of Oakland," a band of middle-class bohemian photographers and artists who went on camping trips to scenic spots in California. A woodstove was provided at this campsite along with what looks like a hand wringer for washing clothes. This view was taken somewhere in the redwoods in 1886.

Oroville (City of Gold) was once the center for a population of Chinese miners, railroad workers, and agricultural laborers reportedly numbering about 10,000. The famous Oroville Chinese Temple was built in 1863 to facilitate the worship of Chinese folk religion, popular religion, Buddhism, Taoism, and Confucianism. Although this photograph, taken on Montgomery Street in Oroville ca. 1890, is labeled as a parade, the presence of several people wearing white robes means this may be a funeral procession.

As in other California cities, Chinese-run businesses in Oroville were housed in the oldest sections of downtown. These shacks are purported to have been the dwelling places of the Chinese residents, and some may have lived in such shanties. They look much like the shacks in the Chinese fishing villages on the Monterey coast. Oroville Chinese also lived in the back rooms and upper stories of commercial buildings and in more conventional housing as well.

Chun Kong You (fourth from left) arrived in Oroville as a railroad worker in 1870. As owner of the Fong Lee (Big Profit) store, which sold herbs and was a licensed gold purchasing agency, he became the most prosperous Chinese businessman in Oroville. His descendants in the Chan family helped preserve the Oroville Chinese Temple, now a museum, in the years following the 1907 flood and are involved with it to this day. Shown here on the Fong Lee porch during Chinese New Year festivities on January 26, 1895, are (from left) Major A. F. Jones, district attorney of Butte County; George C. Perkins, later the 14th governor of California; Major Frank McLaughlin, a well-known mining engineer; Chun Kong You, with an unidentified relative; Chun Suey Yuet, Chun Kong You's adopted daughter; Chun Yip Jen, a Fong Lee partner; R. Milton Greene, an Oroville pharmacist; and David Perkins, brother of George C. Perkins.

This well-dressed young Oroville man might have had this portrait taken to send back to his family in China. He probably worked in the mines or on the railroads. The Chinese population of Oroville largely relocated after a devastating flood in 1907.

Chinese workers thresh lettuce seed in the Salinas Valley in Monterey County, ca. 1900. The recently harvested lettuce field that has been allowed to go to seed can be seen at right, and the workers are beating the seed from the harvested plants with poles. The seed is collected from the tarp below.

Chinese sharecroppers or those with enough land to plant a garden generally sold their vegetables door-to-door, rather than from a fixed place of business. This vegetable peddler was photographed somewhere in the San Francisco Bay Area, ca. 1890. He has set down his burden to let a housewife or cook inspect his produce, which includes apples, celery, grapes, melon, and squash.

A vegetable peddler manages an impressive load while delivering produce to a manicured backyard garden in a wealthy San Francisco neighborhood around 1890. The man on the left wearing an apron, with his traditional braid, or queue, wound about his head, is probably the family cook. The peddler may have his own queue wound inside his hat.

This photograph was taken at the Golden Gate Mine on the Feather River in Butte County in November 1891. Even at this late stage of mining, after hydraulic operations had been outlawed in most of the state, Chinese laborers in traditional clothing can be seen excavating river gravel.

Farmers sometimes preferred the dexterity and skill of Chinese workers for harvesting or processing sensitive crops like olives and lettuce. This photograph, taken between 1900 and 1910, is titled "Olive picking on the Quito Ranch." It was probably taken in the Santa Clara Valley. No traditional Chinese clothing is evident, and a few of these men may have dressed up for the occasion.

This view shows part of Fresno's Chinatown, shaded against the intense Central Valley heat, in 1910. Fresno's Chinatown was established in 1885 and was the multicultural hub of the business district until an economic decline that began in the 1960s left its buildings vacant. Many were demolished. At least one wealthy San Francisco merchant, Lew Kan, had an outlet in Fresno, the Sing Chong Lung Kan Kee Company. Fresno's Chinatown has the oldest Buddhist temple in the valley (at Kern and E streets). A series of brick-walled tunnels runs under this six-block area.

Lok Ting Sue acquired property in the Central Valley railroad town of Hanford from another Chinese resident, Young Chow, and opened an herbal medicine shop he called Sue Chung Kee Store. Soon the alley itself took that name, and only after his death did it become known as China Alley. This is a view of his store and the alley in 1899. L. T. Sue became a famous herbalist who had many patients of all races and was very successful financially. It is estimated that 80 percent of Dr. Sue's patients were Caucasian.

The interior of L. T. Sue's herbal medicine store, known as Sue Chung Kee Store, in Hanford in 1890. L. T. Sue is seated, and his son, Y. T. Sue, is standing. Many of our "wonder drugs" today are synthesized forms of ancient herbal medicines.

The Chinese Center of Knowledge was founded by Y. T. Sue and the Hanford Chinese Association to teach the Chinese language and culture to children of all ages. Pictured here in 1906 is the student body, the Chinese Association, and at left, visiting Hanford High School principal Jacob Neighbor.

Y. T. Sue and his wife pose on a sofa in a Hanford photographer's studio in 1913. This woman is identified as his second wife, who was brought from China as a bride, probably in an arranged marriage. Y. T. Sue, son of famous herbalist L. T. Sue, helped establish the Chinese Center of Knowledge, a one-room school for children of all ages that taught Chinese language and culture after the regular public school hours.

Chinese immigrants from fishing villages founded small communities along the California coast in spots from San Diego to the San Francisco Bay. They processed kelp and helped to develop the squid, abalone, and shrimp industries, harvesting many types of fish. By the late 1880s, there were over 2,000 Chinese living in fishing camps throughout the San Francisco Bay, Monterey, and San Diego areas. This village near Monterey was photographed ca. 1895.

An 1875 guidebook to Monterey states: "Chinatown is distant about one mile from the outskirts of town . . . It is admirably selected for the business carried on by its enterprising citizens—fish curing and abalone shell shipping. Its inhabitants are frugal, industrious and well behaved. Little or no crime occurs among them, and . . . they are a sober, honest set of men, and compare very favorably with their countrymen throughout the State." These fishermen are attaching bait, ca. 1895.

A description dating to 1868 records a Chinese fishing village at Pescadero, Pebble Beach, built directly on the rocks of the seashore. The lateen boats used for fishing were built in San Francisco, and large Chinese junks would anchor off Monterey's Cannery Row, exchanging goods and loading their cargo holds with dried squid for the return trip to China. This shanty in the village at Pebble Beach was photographed ca. 1895.

Chinese fishermen in California hunted for abalone, mussels, oysters, seaweed, shark oil, and shark fin. The majority of their catch was dried for export to China or Hawaii, or transported to San Francisco. Responsible for the growth of the commercial fishing industry in Monterey Bay, Chinese fishermen like the one shown here, ca. 1900, eventually exported 200 to 800 pounds of fresh fish daily to San Francisco when the railroad was built to Monterey. Their use of gill nets and very efficient fishing techniques depleted many species of fish.

Chinese fishermen work in a village at Monterey, ca. 1900. After the 1906 earthquake and fire in San Francisco, some urban Chinese relocated to the fishing village on Point Cabrillo. On May 16, 1906, a fire broke out in a barn and burned most of the village. Many of the villagers then moved back to San Francisco, but some went to McAbee Beach, near Monterey's Cannery Row.

A fisherman strides down a dock in Monterey. As described by J. R. Fitch in the book *Picturesque California*, an 1888 collection edited by John Muir, "The place consists of a double row of shanties, built directly on the rocky shore . . . Everything is unspeakably dirty and redolent with the odor of decaying fish. Swarthy women and little children who are tanned as black as negroes by sun and wind, swarm in the squalid cabins, and tumble about in the dust of the single street. On the rocks about are arranged lattice-work frames that are covered with drying fish."

Founded in the 1850s on Point Alones (or Aulones), and photographed around 1907, this was the largest of the fishing villages along the Monterey coast. It is now the site of Hopkins Marine Station, part of Stanford University.

These children are sitting on the boardwalk in Monterey, ca. 1900. The Chinese fishing villages in Monterey were atypical in having large numbers of women and children. Since large Chinese junks once anchored offshore to exchange goods and load cargo for the return trip to China, one might surmise that some undocumented female passengers might have occasionally disembarked at Monterey in the same manner.

A man standing near a temporary camp in the rocks near Monterey around the turn of the century may be making tea for the fishermen. He carries a kettle in one hand.

The custom of leaving a wife behind in China, the Chinese Exclusion Act passed in 1882, and miscegenation laws contributed to a "bachelor" society of single Chinese men in California that persisted until World War II. This situation sentenced many Chinese men to a lonely life, especially those working in rural areas of California. This lone Chinese worker is carrying an empty set of baskets down a long country road in Palo Alto, ca. 1910.

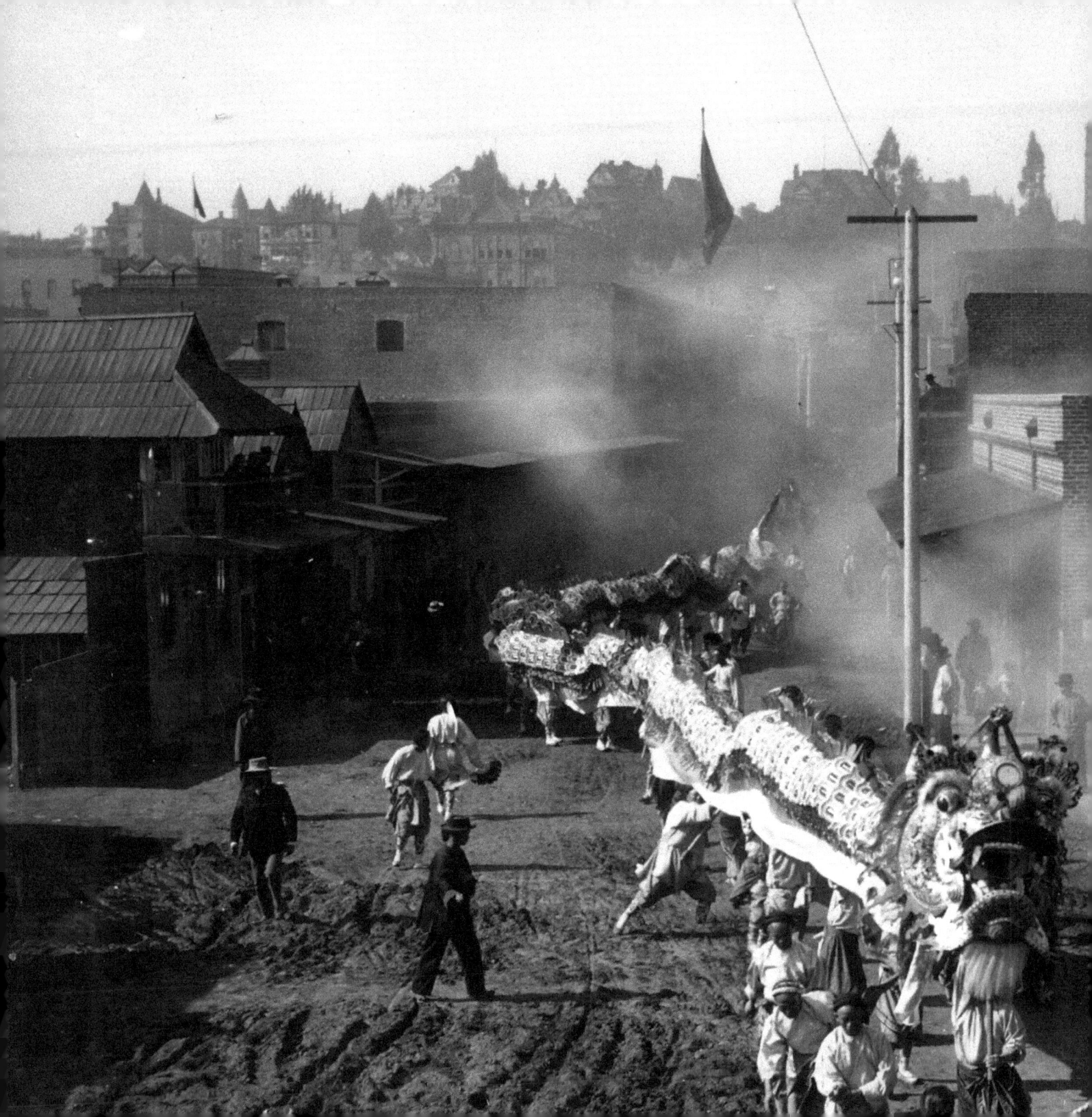

This beautiful dragon deftly avoids a great pothole as it slithers down an unidentified street in Los Angeles's old Chinatown during a New Year's celebration in 1895. The Beacon Hill neighborhood can be seen in the background, and a man on the sidewalk at right may be beating a drum. A permanent Los Angeles Chinese Quarter was established between El Pueblo Plaza and Arcadia Street on Calle de los Negros by 1870. Chinese immigrants had been settling in the city since 1857. When this view was taken, old Chinatown was a bustling district with a population approaching 3,000. Many of the city's earliest commercial buildings were still standing, some of the approximately 200 buildings occupied by Chinese businesses during that era. After 1910, the district declined, losing business to other areas and falling prey to the proliferation of gambling houses, opium dens, and fierce tong warfare during a prolonged period of redevelopment.

The Chinese community participates in La Fiesta de Las Flores in Los Angeles in 1903. This was the year that Theodore Roosevelt attended, and local newspapers portrayed the Chinese as Roosevelt supporters. They also recounted that the Chinese were invited to participate in La Fiesta de Las Flores in the first year it was held, 1897. Although the invitation was controversial, they concluded that the Chinese added a great deal to the fiesta. Not visible in this photograph was a large float that resembled a chariot, and, of course, a hungry dragon.

These two men are drying shrimp and squid on the shore of the San Francisco Bay around 1895. Shrimp camps were scattered at advantageous locations around the Bay, with clusters of camps around Point San Pedro and Point Avisadera, south of the city of San Francisco. According to a map drawn by Robert A. Nash in 1969, there were 17 camps on Point Avisadera alone between 1889 and 1930. The shrimp and squid were brought to market locally or shipped to China, Japan, and the Hawaiian Islands.

Old Chinatown in Los Angeles was at its height when this tourist postcard image was taken on the streets around El Pueblo Plaza, around 1900. The community had survived an era of intense racial hatred and violence. In one horrific incident in 1871, locals slaughtered 19 Chinese. After the turn of the century, a new produce market and new Chinatown would begin to develop, drawing energy and money away from the old plaza.

OLD CHINATOWN

San Francisco was landfall for tens of thousands of Chinese immigrants during the settlement era. Transforming itself from a raucous tent city in 1849 to a famous urban center in a single generation, "Cathay by the Bay" had a distinctly exotic and international character. San Francisco's Chinatown formed quickly near the place where Chinese immigrants first walked on American soil, Portsmouth Plaza (later Portsmouth Square). It became the largest Chinese community in the nation.

Beginning with a series of shops along Sacramento Street, Chinese merchants filled up older structures vacated as white businessmen rushed to the wharves and streets built on landfill. Here Chinese merchants prospered by providing new arrivals with equipment, loans, advice, and employment. They could speak their own language and be understood. They could find familiar food. They could gamble, drink, and smoke opium to ease pain and homesickness. They could worship their gods and honor their ancestors openly.

In the 1850s, wealthy merchants established benevolent associations based on province or surname. They joined together to become the Chinese Consolidated Benevolent Association, also known as the Chinese Six Companies, which not only negotiated with local government officials, but was authorized to represent the Chinese throughout the United States. Wisely the Companies worked through Caucasian attorneys who were completely versed in the technicalities of Western law.

Discriminatory laws ensured that few Chinese women could immigrate, and most of the first brave female argonauts became prostitutes. Young Chinese bachelors, not unlike their white counterparts, frequented opium dens and brothels, and some merchants became rich supporting this trade. But as more merchants and a few other fortunate men retrieved or ordered brides from China, a growing number of schools, theaters, and joss houses appeared. Protestant missionaries sought to assimilate Chinatown's children and assail its vices by establishing Christian missionary schools.

By 1886 Chinatown was a densely populated commercial area bounded by Stockton, California, Kearny, and Washington streets, and anchored by Portsmouth Square. Its appeal to white tourists and photographers was already magnetic, mixing fear with fascination. With its residents forbidden to live or stray outside its boundaries by the city that surrounded it, Chinatown became a world unto itself, a citadel of an ancient culture developing a colony in a new world.

The population of the Chinese district in San Francisco may have been more dispersed in the first decade after the gold rush. This very early view, taken in 1858, is labeled, "Alley off Post Street between Grant Avenue and Kearny Street." At that time Grant would have been called Dupont Street. The only existing alley that now fits that description is Robert Kirk Lane. This location would have been outside the boundaries of Chinatown, but may have had housing for immigrants.

An 1859 view of the south side of Sacramento Street west of Kearny Street shows an early location of Hop Yik & Company, owned by influential merchant Wen Cheong Ngan. To the right is the Broderick Fire Engine Company (named after David C. Broderick) sporting an American eagle. St. Mary's Cathedral can be seen in the background. Note the cellar door and planked streets.

Sacramento Street filled with shops and markets run by Chinese as other merchants moved closer to the wharf and commercial areas built on landfill. Chy Lung & Company, located at 640 Sacramento Street, is shown here in 1866. It was founded by merchant Lai Chu-chuen in 1850. He became an influential importer of Chinese laborers and owned railroad stock in addition to offering tea, opium, silk, lacquered goods, and groceries. The founder died in 1869, but his store continued to thrive until 1912.

Balconies with potted rose bushes grace Dupont Street (later Grant Avenue) in 1866. Hop Kee & Company (center) was owned by Cnang Hung. Hop Yik & Company (right) was owned by Wen Cheong Ngan. This was either a new location for the Hop Yik & Company store on Sacramento Street, or an additional outlet. According to the *Daily Alta California* newspaper, both men were prominent businessmen who mixed with state officials. Hop Kee & Company also funded the transport of the first Chinese immigrants to Victoria, Canada, in 1858, and imported 2,000 pounds of Hong Kong opium to San Francisco in 1880.

Onlookers at right seem to be gazing down Sacramento Street toward the bay, and the sky seems filled with smoke or clouds in this view published in 1866, long before the great earthquake and fire of 1906. Here the first Chinese district has board sidewalks crowded with merchandise. In the tradition of outdoor markets in China, merchants brought their wares out from behind the confines of the Western store display window.

Chinatown residents called Sacramento Street Tong Yun Gai, or Street of the Chinese, the new headquarters of the Chinese in America. Captured here in 1865, the cluttered sidewalks catered to the immigrants' every need, from food to footwear to fortune-telling.

Bartlett Alley, off Washington Street, was a particular favorite for photographers in the late 1800s. The elaborate round window at right on the upper floor is a unique feature that appears in many photographs.

Wells Fargo and Company moved into the building at the northwest corner of California and Montgomery streets after the financial panic of 1855. According to historian Thomas W. Chinn, this building, built in 1852 and shown here in 1866, had its granite blocks precut in China. Chinese masons in San Francisco discovered that according to *feng shui*, the building had been designed for the opposite corner, and they refused to build it at the inauspicious site. American contractors completed the structure, and Adams and Company Express occupied it. Rival firm Wells Fargo occupied another stone building on the opposite corner. The Chinese gold miners and merchants favored Wells Fargo, and it was partially their patronage and imperturbable refusal to withdraw their money that made Wells Fargo one of the few businesses to survive the panic. Wells Fargo took over the building when Adams and Company failed, finally appeasing the spirits.

A horse makes a turn heading down the alley at Washington Place, labeled here as the "Heart of Chinatown," ca. 1892. The original stereograph of this image was subtitled in German, a testament to the international appeal of San Francisco's Chinatown.

Pedestrians throng Dupont Street (later Grant Avenue) in the 1880s. There appears to be an equal mix of Chinese and other ethnic groups along these busy sidewalks.

The solemn gaze of this girl seems appropriate for her tiny bound feet. The origin of this painful custom is uncertain, but most authorities trace it to the T'ang dynasty (618–907 A.D.). An early account describes shoes with upturned toes worn by dancers in the royal court that resembled lotus flowers. Bound feet were a mark of aristocracy, indicating that these women could neither work nor walk long distances. Consequently very few Chinese women in California had bound feet.

Chinatown's telephone exchange is seen here with its first operator, ca. 1894. The first public pay telephone in Chinatown was installed in 1891, and three years later a small switchboard began operation to serve Chinese-speaking subscribers. Operators knew several dialects and each customer by name, so numbers were unnecessary. They could even distinguish between subscribers of the same name.

These extremely well-dressed Chinese pedestrians, seen on what appears to be Kearny Street, were not a common sight outside Chinatown. Since the image is thought to be of four women, one wonders if there is a man just out of camera range escorting them to some special destination, perhaps the California Mid-winter International Exposition in 1894. Chinese women who were not prostitutes or laborers were generally not allowed to walk the streets unescorted except for one day, the Festival of the Good Lady.

This family group in Golden Gate Park was photographed in the 1890s. Their silk robes and embroidered slippers are worthy of a very special occasion. Since it was rare to see Chinese women outside of their homes, it is fair to speculate that this family was resting during a visit to the California Mid-winter International Exposition in 1894.

Carrying burdens that belie their youth, these girls are well dressed and groomed as they wait in the cobblestone streets.

The Presbyterian Mission hosted this elaborate wedding, ca. 1896. Shown left to right are the best man, groom, servant, bride, brother, two sisters, parents, and child servant. Some of the party were students of Donaldina Cameron, who came to Chinatown's Presbyterian-run Occidental Mission Home for Girls in 1895 to teach sewing to Asian women, but ended up saving more than 3,000 women and children from the slavery of forced prostitution and servitude during her 40 years there. The Occidental Mission Home was later renamed the Donaldina Cameron House.

An elaborately decorated Chinese pharmacy in Chinatown has meticulously arrayed herbal medicines, while the owner and his son pose. According to information that accompanied this photograph when it was exhibited in the Crocker-Anglo Bank, the image was taken in 1895. An 1856 Chinese business directory for San Francisco already listed 15 Oriental pharmacies. A Chinese prescription usually contained many herbs, roots, nuts, or flowers imported from China.

On October 18, 1852, Tong Hook Tong mounted the first Cantonese opera on a San Francisco stage at the American Theatre on Sansome Street. Several months later, the first Chinese theater building was completed. The theater shown here, on Jackson Street, around 1897, could seat several hundred. Women occupied the curtained loges, and workers sat on wooden benches, the box seats reserved for the wealthy merchants who ruled Chinatown. Typically there were no female performers, drop curtains, flies, or wings to allow actors to exit. They entered and exited from doors in the rear.

Children in holiday clothing play with a balloon from a street vendor, ca. 1898. Cherished children were allowed to play on the sidewalks and stoops of Chinatown. With no formal playground until 1927, children were tolerated and cared for by all.

Dupont Street, later renamed Grant Avenue, is seen here from Clay Street in 1900. The Chinese transliteration of the name is Dupon Gai, meaning "slatboard capital street." Early photographs show Sacramento Street paved in wooden planks, and early Dupont Street may have been as well. Dupont gradually siphoned off business from the original Chinese Quarter on Sacramento Street. By the time this shot was taken, the streets and sidewalks had been paved. The balconied buildings hung with lanterns were a favorite of photographers.

Lee Tung Hay, one of the lucky few, was able to bring his wife, Lee Mon Jeong, from China and raise a family in nineteenth-century Oakland. In this 1891 photo, ten-year-old Charles Lee (back row, middle) poses with his family in traditional clothing. Charles became the first Chinese dentist in California, practicing for 34 years in Oakland before retiring in 1940. He helped start the Oakland Lodge of the Chinese American Citizens' Alliance and was active in other community groups. His son, Lester, became an Oakland dentist too.

A permanent East Bay Chinatown was established at Eighth and Webster streets in Oakland in the 1870s. This postcard photo of Oakland's Chinatown, taken ca. 1900, shows a less urban environment than San Francisco's Chinatown. No doubt some Chinese immigrants, just like their European counterparts, preferred the East Bay, where there was more open land and sunshine, and less fog. In 1869 Oakland became the terminus of the of the Central Pacific (later Southern Pacific) Railroad, which provided work for the Chinese and many others as Oakland grew into an industrial center. The Chinese could also find work on the farms and dairies that once surrounded Oakland.

Made for sale to tourists, this postcard stresses that this is a "typical" scene in the Chinese quarter of Oakland, expressing a general anthropological interest, rather than identifying a particular street or store. Judging by the clothing worn, it was taken around 1900. Produce and jars of what may be herbal medicines are displayed in front of the store.

Business names appearing in this photo of a commercial block in Oakland's Chinatown are (left to right): Sheng Ho & Co. (awning), Quong Shew & Company General Merchandise, Yuen Hung Low Restaurant, and Yuen Fong Low Restaurant. "Sheng" could mean birth or to live, and "Ho" means peace. The way these words are written indicate that they are Cantonese. The Chinese letters on the windows repeat the name of the shop in Cantonese. Chinese restaurants, offering savory meat and nutritious vegetable dishes, were an immediate success throughout the state from the earliest days of the gold rush. Here two Chinese restaurants operate side by side.

This postcard image shows a large commercial store in Oakland's Chinatown, ca. 1900. According to author William Wong, there were three earlier Chinese districts in Oakland: at First and Castro streets, Telegraph Avenue between Sixteenth and Seventeenth streets, and San Pablo Avenue between Nineteenth and Twentieth streets. Targeted by hostile neighbors, these Chinese districts did not last, and one mysteriously burned. It is the Chinatown shown here near Eighth and Webster streets that endured and still exists today. A small sign on the second story of this building can be transliterated as *yuong li,* which is the Mandarin pronunciation of words that mean something like forever prosperous.

A Salvation Army rescue worker leads children past an herbal medicine store in San Francisco's Chinatown, ca. 1900. The Salvation Army first came to Chinatown in 1886, and like the Presbyterian Mission, rescued orphaned or abandoned children. It continues to serve congregations in Chinatown today.

These may be children under the care of the Salvation Army rescue team, with their caregiver shown at left. The children stand outside a toy store in Chinatown, ca. 1900, wearing a mix of Western and Oriental clothing.

Festivities surrounding Chinese New Year in San Francisco included traditional colors, decorations, flowers, and fruits that symbolize good fortune and wealth. This photo, taken around 1900, is titled "The Lily Vendor," referring to the flower known as the Chinese Sacred Lily (Narcissus tazetta orientalis), often forced for winter bloom. Legend claims these bulbs came with the first Chinese immigrants to the United States. Technically they are not in the lily family; nor did they originate in China, but traveled along the Silk Road from Spain.

This vendor weighed down by overflowing baskets appears to be carrying Chinese Sacred Lilies and other produce as well. San Francisco passed several discriminatory local laws aimed at stifling competition from Chinese launderers and vegetable peddlers. General Order 976, amended December 19, 1870, stated: "No person upon any sidewalk shall carry a basket or baskets, bag or bags, suspended from or attached to poles across or upon the shoulders."

A wealthy man, perhaps a local merchant, walks with his child down a Chinatown street at the turn of the century. Stacked on the sidewalk are the ubiquitous all-purpose barrels and buckets of old Chinatown.

The charm of ornate, Italianate building facades with decorated wrought-iron balconies hung with lanterns helped make turn-of-the-century Chinatown an international tourist destination. Banners on the building at center indicate it was a hotel and restaurant. Yet overcrowding is also evident by the fence between the buildings seen in this photograph, a sign that the roof area is in use and must be protected from intruders. The roofs of Chinatown were often used to dry fish and other foods, even up until modern times.

Variously titled "The Mountebank," "The Pekin [sic] Two Knife Man," and "The Sword Dancer," this image is actually a portrait of Sung Chi Liang, who practiced martial arts of the Old Empire. Performing in the streets of Chinatown, he was nicknamed Big Ox for his strength. He also sold an herbal medicine, *tit daa yeuk jau,* used to heal bruises, hence the term mountebank, meaning huckster. He was photographed in front of 32–34 Waverly Place.

This "slave girl in holiday attire" walks at the intersection of Dupont (now Grant Avenue) and Jackson streets, ca. 1900. According to author John Kuo Wei Tchen, she was a beautiful and popular prostitute. Sold into service by their families, Chinese girls were kidnapped and forced into prostitution to serve the needs of the bachelor society brought about by both Chinese culture in America and the discriminatory Chinese Exclusion Act. A few, like this woman, may have enjoyed fine food and clothing, but for most it was a squalid, hard life, fraught with disease and early death.

This image, taken ca. 1900, is titled "Street of the Gamblers." Former chief of police Jesse B. Cook estimated in his account "San Francisco's Old Chinatown" that there were about 62 lottery agents, 50 fan tan games, and 8 lottery drawings in Chinatown in 1889. He described the gambling establishments as protected by elaborate systems of lookouts and three-door passageways, "so that if the police got through the first door, they had to pass through a second door, which, of course, would be locked. By the time they finally got to the game room, all evidence would be removed."

The proprietor of a Chinatown shop poses outside his doorway around 1900. The items for sale are small, and may be medicinal.

Residents of Chinatown often got their news by reading bulletins posted on certain walls. Crowds would be drawn to hear about momentous events, especially those concerning China.

A group of men watches for newly posted bulletins on the progress of the Boxer Rebellion in 1901, an attempt by the Qing dynasty to oust foreigners and their influences in China. Boxer fighters, believing in their own supernatural powers, besieged foreign embassies and missionaries until the Boxers were defeated by the Eight Nation Alliance (Austria-Hungary, France, Germany, Italy, Japan, Russia, the United Kingdom, and the United States). Allied troops then commenced a vengeful campaign that ended on September 7, 1901. The rebellion greatly weakened the Qing dynasty, setting the stage for the 1911 Revolution.

Typical of the photographs taken for the tourist trade, this one is labeled simply "A Chinese family." Taken in San Francisco by William Henry Jackson, ca. 1900, for his Detroit Photographic Company, the spare title indicates a generic anthropological interest in these "exotic" subjects, similar to the titles given to photographs of the American Indian.

In 1860 the California legislature decreed that white children should be educated separately from Indian, African American, and Chinese children. In 1884, when Chinese immigrants Joseph and Mary Tape challenged the law by trying to enroll their daughter, Mamie, in a San Francisco public school, the State Supreme Court ruled in the Tapes' favor. But citing a "separate but equal" doctrine, the San Francisco School Board established an all-Asian public school, shown here ca. 1900, that Mamie and all other Chinese children were forced to attend.

No one ever doubted that Chinatown residents treasured their children. Photographers both before and after the 1906 earthquake recorded scores of children playing or tagging along after their parents. Despite the specter of female sexual and domestic slavery and the dangers of the streets, these stoops and curbs were a safe playground for more than one generation. In this view ca. 1903, entitled "A New Toy," a child wonders at a street vendor's merchandise.

The subjects of this 1904 photograph were well known in Chinatown. Lew Kan was a Chinese labor contractor for the Alaskan canneries and he owned a store at 714 Sacramento Street called Fook On Lung, and later another in Fresno, the Sing Chong Lung Kan Kee Company. His height, over six feet, was only exceeded by his wealth. His sons, Lew Bing You (center) and Lew Bing Yuen (right) wear satin and velvet suits with double mushroom designs, symbolizing the scepter of Buddha and long life.

Isaiah West Taber photographed this butcher shop and its handsome butcher (perhaps the owner of the shop) several times. Here the butcher gazes directly and proudly at the camera. The shop is an example of the sidewalk market style of China, which was so prevalent in Chinatown but not in other commercial districts in the city. Here meat and produce are arrayed outdoors to attract the attention of pedestrians.

Taber photographed the same butcher shop later the same day, the proprietors now peering from behind their groceries with their stores diminished by a day of sales. Anti-Chinese sentiment was rampant at this time, and several local laws were passed to suppress Chinese competition in the marketplace.

A woman in dark, utilitarian clothing is carrying an infant who is gorgeously attired in Imperial dress. She is apparently walking unescorted down a main thoroughfare, probably Sacramento Street, before the 1906 earthquake and fire. A guess is that this is a servant transporting the child of an aristocrat in Chinatown, perhaps a merchant. Women were rarely seen alone on the streets outside of their homes.

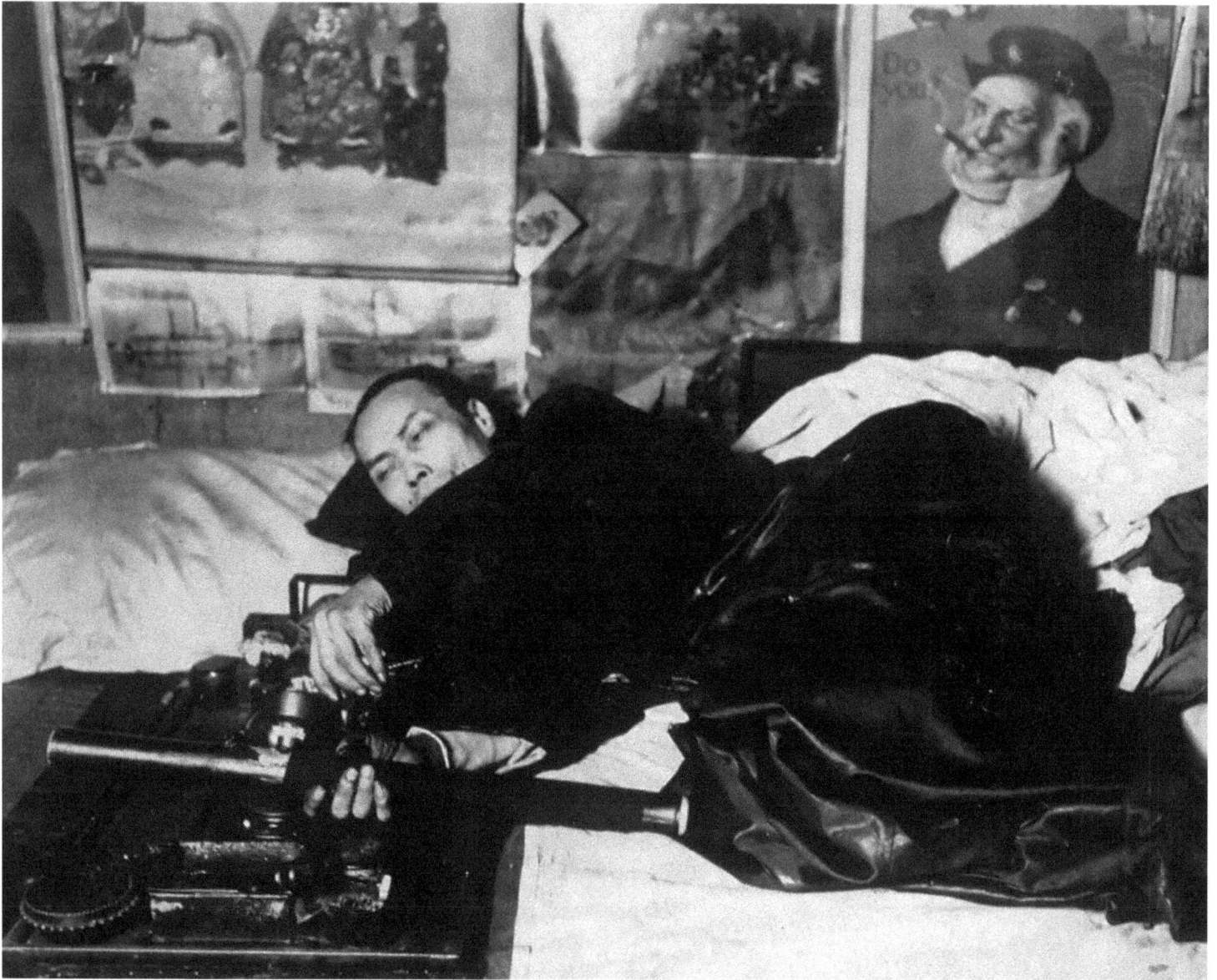

Opium importation and use was an accepted part of Chinese culture, and this acceptance transferred to early California. Some merchants became wealthy importing opium in large amounts. Forced into an overcrowded ghetto and lacking the support of families, single men found solace in the opium pipe. Although Westerners used opiates in a liquid form known as laudanum or paragoric, opium smoking was viewed with equal parts disgust and fascination by most Caucasians. Many tourists visited these "dens" to inhale that peculiar, sweet smell.

According to San Francisco's former chief of police Jesse B. Cook, "The opium den was . . . resorted to because they had no other place to go." Most of the stores in Chinatown had back-room opium dens that could accommodate as many as 100, Cook recalled. "In those days the Chinese were allowed to smoke opium, provided they did not do so in the presence of a white man," he noted, adding, "the smoke was sometimes so thick in those dens that the gas jets looked like small matches burning."

The opium trade was taken over by tongs, or criminal gangs, that were not routed out of Chinatown until the 1920s. Yet photographers continued to be drawn to the romance of the drug and the culture that produced it. Photographer Charles Weidner photographed a very similar scene at this same doorway, perhaps on the same day, in 1900, entitled "Hitting the Pipe."

Chinatown, constrained by local laws that prohibited Chinese from owning land outside its boundaries, crammed 22,000 people and all the stores, services, and institutions they needed into a 12-block area by 1885. In 1880, the ratio of men to women was 20 to 1, and by about 1905, when this photograph was taken, Chinatown was still mostly a male enclave.

This funeral procession, probably along Dupont Street (now Grant Avenue), ca. 1905, includes a horse-drawn hearse and Buddhist monks. Prominent citizens of Chinatown were accorded elaborate funeral processions. Perhaps the largest funeral ever held in Chinatown was for Tom Kim Yung, visiting Chinese legation military attaché to the United States in 1903. Yung committed suicide after losing face because of a scuffle with police. Apparently it was completely the fault of the police, a case of mistaken identity.

A funeral feast is set out on a Chinatown street, ca. 1904, while both Orientals and Occidentals observe. The priest or mourner wears a white headband, a color used exclusively for funerals. The funeral feast probably included a whole roasted pig and a chicken or duck on wooden trays. Other delicacies like dumplings or fruit or cakes would be added to the feast.

At this burial site in Colma, just south of San Francisco, ca. 1903, the food from the funeral feast is left on the grave to supply the departed with sustenance for the "dragon trip" to the land of total bliss.

Organized in 1880 by Dr. Jesse B. Hartwell, the Chinese Baptist congregation met in a storefront on Washington Street across from Portsmouth Square until this building was erected in 1888. The church at Waverly Place and Sacramento Street is shown here shortly before the earthquake. It served the established Chinese community and newcomers, and an essential part of its mission was to teach students who originally were not allowed to attend public school. It provided a day school and Chinese language school staffed by missionaries, and an adult night school to teach English.

Following spread: The celestial magic of Old Dupont Street (now Grant Avenue) is captured in this rare night scene, probably taken not long before the 1906 earthquake. Fire soon swept this street clean of the charming, rickety balconies hung with glowing lanterns.

After the 1906 earthquake and fire, many photographers cashed in on the nostalgia for old Chinatown by reproducing their pre-earthquake views to sell. This image, copyrighted in 1907, shows a pre-1906 view of Washington Place.

NEW CHINATOWN

The San Francisco earthquake of April 18, 1906, and its fiery aftermath turned old Chinatown, home to an estimated 14,000 people, into a muddy mash of crusted pottery, ash, twisted metal, and an untold number of charred bodies. Many Chinese never came back to the ruins, settling instead in Oakland or other urban Chinatowns. At the time many San Franciscans would have been happy to see the Chinese relocated to the Hunter's Point mudflats. Chinatown had survived earlier eradication attempts and intermittent violence from its neighbors. Although a Reconstruction Committee presented a relocation plan, Chinatown's Chinese Six Companies, the Empress of China, and the hope of tax revenues from tourists and Chinese stores convinced city officials to allow Chinatown to rise again at the same location.

A farsighted second-generation Chinese American, Look Tin Eli, convinced other merchants to follow his plan and hire American architects to redesign their buildings to look like Chinese buildings in order to attract tourists. His store, the Sing Chong Bazaar on Grant Avenue, and the many other structures that imitated it were not strictly Chinese architecture. They represented the prevalent American "modern" commercial architecture of the era with a frosting of decorative Oriental elements, including curved eaves, ornate balconies, and pagoda roofs. Like Look Tin Eli himself, this new Chinatown was a sometimes perplexing mix of traditional Chinese culture, American ambition, and commercial savvy.

Even more importantly for the future of new Chinatown, virtually all of the city's birth records had been destroyed. Chinese men could now claim citizenship and therefore the right to bring their families from China. Soon Chinatown residents returned with what were called "paper sons and daughters," whose paternity was suspect. Yet for the first time the balance of men and women in Chinatown began to equalize and middle-class families became common, a change that had far-reaching social and cultural impact.

Responding to the proliferation of "paper sons," and expecting a flood of new immigration after the completion of the Panama Canal, the federal government built Angel Island Immigration Station. Hundreds of thousands of Asian immigrants passed through Angel Island before it closed its doors in 1940. The Chinese Exclusion Act was repealed in 1943, and finally, in 1965, the government abolished quota systems based on national origin.

In the early morning of April 18, 1906, the earth shook for less than one minute, yet the aftermath would soon destroy much of a great city and virtually all of Chinatown. Here people have gathered in the intersections of Sacramento Street and are gazing transfixed at the approaching fire, feeling safe enough to bring out chairs, as the group of Chinese men at right have done, rather than fleeing for their lives. With most water mains broken by the shaking, there would be no stopping the inferno.

Included in a collection of San Francisco earthquake images, this one shows a group of aristocratic children walking down an unidentified street, perhaps fleeing to safer ground. One young man looks fearfully behind him, even as a nonchalant Western businessman strolls by with his briefcase.

As the smoke finally began to clear after the earthquake and fire, photographers made it to the scene of the horrifying destruction. Here the view is down Sacramento Street, where acres of rubble and melted, twisted iron filled the street that once had such charm. The official city estimate of 400 dead is thought to be unreliable, and researchers have placed the figure at approximately 3,000.

It is not known how many Chinese died in those blocks crammed with people and merchandise, where even the rooftops were used. It is estimated that 14,000 lived there at the turn of the century. Here in the smoke of an artificial dusk in April 1906, a stricken Chinese man stands amidst the ruins of what may once have been his home.

The ruins of the Chinese Baptist Church rise starkly above the rubble after the fire has devastated the street. With the help of American Baptists across the country, a new building was erected in 1908, with the ground floor housing a sanctuary and a reading room, and the second floor serving as classrooms.

Even the narrow alleys of Chinatown had reappeared by the time this photograph was taken in 1908, although devoid of the charming balconies and overhangs of old Chinatown. Here Spofford Alley is decorated for the Moon Festival. In Chinese celestial cosmology, the moon represents the female principle, or yin. Only women took part in Moon Festival rituals on the night of the full moon. Altars would be set up in households, and when the full moon appeared, women would make offerings of incense, candles, fruit, flowers, and mooncakes. But here the festivities have spilled outdoors.

The new buildings in Chinatown rose quickly from the ashes, with utilitarian fire escapes on their facades instead of wrought-iron balconies and pedimented Italianate windows. These Chinese priests stride down a street in Chinatown around 1910.

A Chinese cemetery existed at one time adjacent to Chinatown between California Street and Geary Boulevard. It was later moved. With the population explosion in full swing throughout San Francisco, and with the increase in the cost of land, city fathers took action by passing Bill No. 54 and Ordinance No. 25 on March 26, 1900, stating that no further burials would be allowed in the city and county of San Francisco. The city of Colma became the new location for the Chinese cemetery seen here, ca. 1910.

After the original Chinese telephone exchange was destroyed in the earthquake and fire, another was built on Washington Street, between Brenham Place and Grant Avenue. This ornate interior shows that at least some of the operators at this time were women.

After the original telephone exchange building was destroyed, the present building was constructed under the direction of the manager, Kum Shu Loo, on Washington Street. When he died in 1926, his son, Kern Loo, took over and kept that job until he died in 1947. At the height of its operations, the telephone exchange had 2,477 subscribers. In 1949, the Pacific Telephone and Telegraph Company switched to the dial system, so the telephone exchange went out of business and the building was sold.

Early in Chinatown's history, benevolent associations formed based on the last name or home district of the new arrivals. The purpose of these associations was to protect and help kin or neighbors in a new land to find employment, settle disputes, provide burials, and so forth. Six of these associations (Ning Yuen, Hop Wo, Kong Chow, Yeung Wo, Sam Yup, and Yan Wo, with Sue Hing added later) came together in the 1850s as the Chinese Consolidated Benevolent Association, more commonly known as the Chinese Six Companies. The officers are shown here, ca. 1910.

The Chinese Six Companies constituted a powerful political group, made up almost exclusively of wealthy Chinatown merchants. They became the mouthpiece and representatives of the Chinese in the United States. Wisely working through a Caucasian attorney, the Six Companies eventually influenced city, state, and national policy regarding immigration, and broadcast their communications to the world at large. Shown here is the new headquarters of the Chinese Six Companies around 1910.

The Man Fung Wo butcher and grocery store at 921 Dupont Street (now Grant Avenue), pictured here in 1908, has an advertising banner that indicates the store also carried herbal medicines. The outdoor Chinese market style persisted after the earthquake and fire resettlement.

Most Chinatown residents lost everything in the great fire of 1906, but one disaster worked to their advantage: the records and vital statistics at city hall had been incinerated as well. They could now claim U.S. citizenship, and no one could prove otherwise. They could legally return to China to retrieve their families. Some returned with many "paper sons and daughters," who became instant citizens. The bachelor society of Chinatown began to equalize, and children, like these youngsters in Portsmouth Square enjoying a puppet show ca. 1910, were not the rarity that they had once been.

Partially in response to the proliferation of "paper sons and daughters" after the earthquake and fire destroyed citizenship records, the government opened Angel Island Immigration Station in 1910 to enforce the exclusion act of 1882. It was built at a place once called China Cove because of an old Chinese fishing camp. This view shows the debarking pier, the first landfall for immigrants, with the main buildings at center and right, and the hospital at left.

Although officials thought the station would also handle a flood of European immigrants after the completion of the Panama Canal, Angel Island actually processed a majority of Asians. The Chinese were detained longest at the station, anywhere from two weeks to twenty-two months. Family members were separated and interrogated in isolation. Anxiety was high, for an incorrect answer could mean they were denied admission. This is a view of the examination room.

Because of Angel Island's treatment of Asian immigrants, keeping them for weeks or months when European immigrants at Ellis Island were only detained for hours or days, some view it as having been a detention center. Angel Island was the first stop for 250,000 Chinese immigrants before it closed in 1940. This is a view of the immigration station kitchen that fed those housed in dormitories on the island while they were detained.

The Chinese had their own names for all of Chinatown's streets and alleys. The Chinese named Spofford Alley, shown here, Sun Louie Sun Hong, or New Spanish Alley, referring to the Mexican Californians who once lived there. Ross Alley was known as Gow Louie Sun Hong, or Old Spanish Alley. It is adorned with the flags of the new Republic of China, ca. 1913. Note the war gods guarding the doorway at left, which may be an entrance to a joss house. This alley was rumored to be a stronghold of Dr. Sun Yat-sen's revolutionaries.

The Cathay Chinese Boys Band was founded in October 1911 by a group of 12 boys (aged 9 to 16) inspired by the Columbia Park Boys Band, another marching band in San Francisco. Funded by the Chinese Six Companies, they became the first Chinese band in America. For their inspired cross-cultural performances, they used Chinese instruments to play American tunes, and American instruments to play Chinese music. Starting out in drab gray military uniforms for participating in funerals, they later donned flashy costumes for performances throughout the United States and almost every important local event. The musicians' union pressed local mortuaries to hire union bands for the steady funeral work, and so the Boys Band was forced into retirement in 1962. Thomas Lyn, later to become president of the club, is seated third from right.

The Chinatown Knights, Chinatown's first modern jazz orchestra, pose here on May 30, 1935. Philip P. Choy traced the history of the Knights and the Cathayans, descendants of the Cathay Chinese Boys Band. The Knights had crossover membership with the earlier band, and both were formed in response to the discriminatory constraints that kept these talented young musicians out of mainstream orchestras until the 1950s. The Knights were a fixture in Chinatown and played venues like the St. Francis Hotel. The members shown here are Harry Wong, Andrew Wong, Henry Leong, Thomas Wu, Jack Wong, and Billy Leong.

The Cathay Chinese Boys Band may be somewhere in this long Chinese New Year's Parade moving down Van Ness Avenue in 1912. Chinese New Year is a two-week spring festival that has been celebrated for over 5,000 years in China. The New Year's Parade in San Francisco began in the 1860s and has grown to become the largest Asian event in North America. The Golden Dragon, a creature endowed with awesome powers, leads the procession. This mythical dragon is the source of the elements and the custodian of the seasons, as well as the source of life and prosperity. Those who touch him are blessed.

Rising from the ashes of 1906, "Cathay by the Bay" was ready to throw open its doors to the world at the Panama Pacific International Exposition of 1915. This view shows the ground-breaking for the Chinese Pagoda, ca. 1913, one of five structures modeled after originals in the Forbidden City and built by native artisans transported from China. China's participation in the exposition was more extensive and expensive than any other foreign nation.

Chinese musical theater was performed in the Chinese Village at the Panama Pacific International Exposition. This is a scene from a Chinese drama with elaborate stage sets and props.

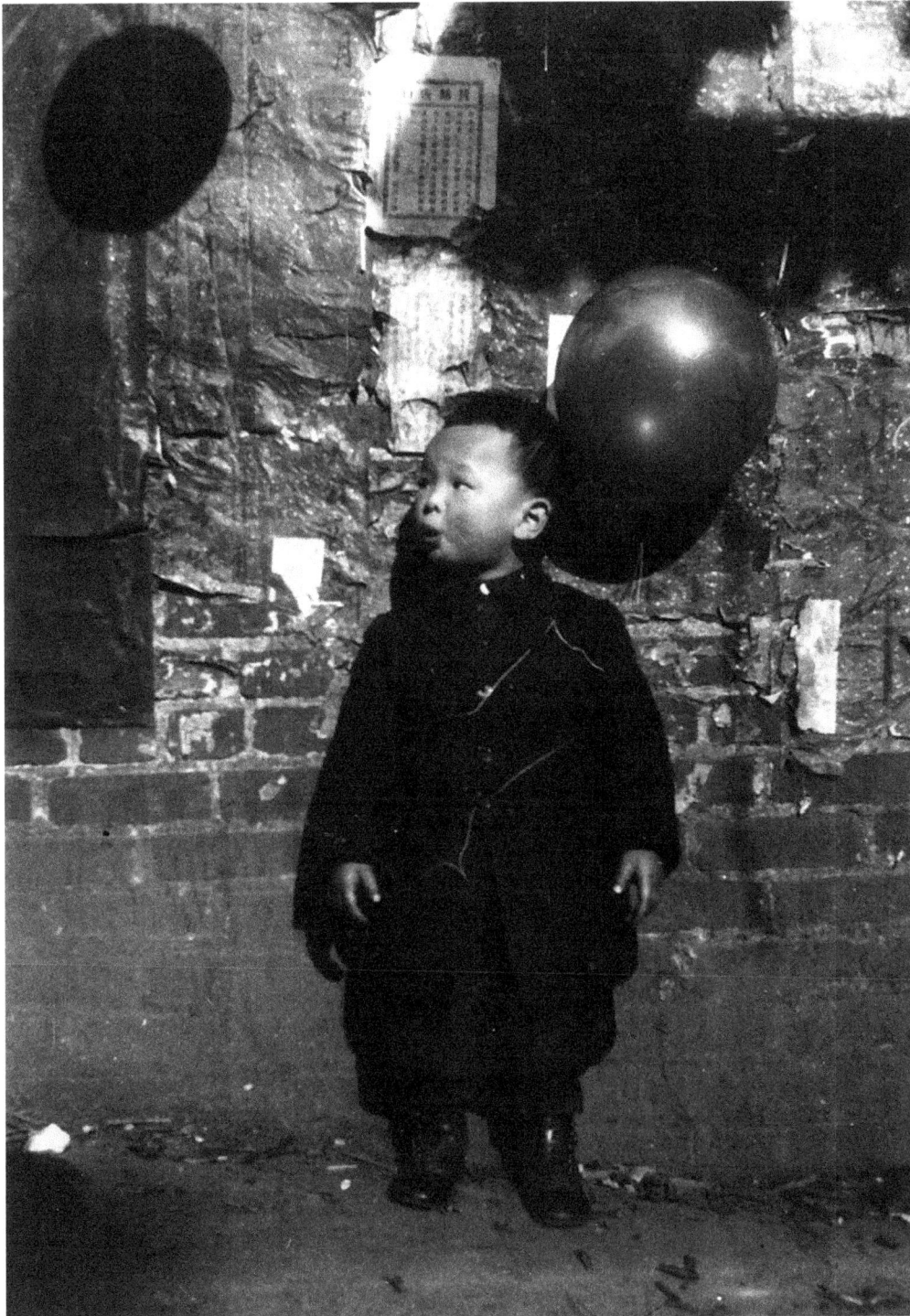

After Sun Yat-sen led the revolution that overthrew the Qing dynasty on October 10, 1911, creating the new Republic of China, many cultural changes were absorbed by the Chinese Californians. Louis Wang, seen here, is not wearing the silk Imperial garb often seen on children in old Chinatown. Gazing at nearby balloons, his own string wound around his coat, he looks like a miniature Sun Yat-sen, wearing the same black wool coat as the revered leader of the Republic.

It is not entirely clear what is transpiring in this unusual view of a fireworks display in Chinatown around 1915. The men on the balcony above are holding ropes that lead to the sidewalk below. They may be lighting the fireworks and then lowering them into the street. This could be a celebration of Double Ten Day, honoring the birth of the Republic of China and held annually in San Francisco since 1911 on or about October 10.

A young man with wheels has the run of Chinatown streets, ca. 1915. Still confined to an area of less than 20 square blocks, the children of Chinatown knew the territory and often played on the stoops and sidewalks of this virtual village.

Once rarely seen on Chinatown's streets, working-class families were a common sight by 1915. The destruction of birth records in the 1906 earthquake and fire made it possible for many Chinatown residents to claim citizenship and retrieve wives and family from China. Here a mother helps her children look into the satchel of a balloon vendor who is not Chinese. Perhaps they are picking out a favorite color for their balloon.

A man roasts chestnuts on a Chinatown sidewalk around 1915. Following the example of citizens of the new Republic of China, most Chinese in California cut off the long braid, or queue, after 1911 and adopted Western dress. It is unclear whether this man has removed his queue, or merely has it wound under his hat. The clothing of the boys in the background is indistinguishable from that of their Italian, Greek, or American neighbors.

Chinese boys, all in modern Western clothing, play in the cobbled streets of Chinatown in the late afternoon sun. An older man in more traditional Chinese clothing looks up from the street in the background. Assimilation was under way for the second generation in Chinatown.

In old Chinatown the merchants brought their wares and produce outdoors on the sidewalk, and in new Chinatown the sidewalk vendor appeared. This man sold oranges, apples, bananas, tobacco, and other items. At the end of the day, his stand could be covered and cleverly locked away.

A lovely young woman tends her infant, who holds a piece of fruit, protected lovingly from the grime of the sidewalk by an unfolded newspaper, ca. 1915.

This working-class Chinese patriarch proudly poses with his growing family, ca. 1915. Judging by the ages of his children, he was probably a bachelor before the 1906 earthquake. Once the privilege of the merchant class, large families quickly became the norm, adding to the overcrowding of Chinatown. These children are dressed in a mixture of Western and Oriental fashions, indicating that Chinatown was slowly becoming the cultural melting pot that was for so long prevented by segregation and discrimination. Some think this baby observes his father's smoking habit with marked disapproval.

Chinese women once spent their lives serving the needs of their fathers, brothers, or husbands. Many early arrivals in San Francisco were forced into servitude, domestic slavery, or prostitution. Although more numerous and less abused than their pioneer counterparts, young women in early twentieth century Chinatown still led very circumscribed lives, often in the background of social life. This young lady wears holiday attire while gazing from the balcony of a temple on California Street.

The blank brick walls of Ross Alley seem adorned only by fire escapes and doorways as a lone pedestrian makes his way past them toward the sunlight, ca. 1915. This is in sharp contrast to the bustling, balconied alleyways of old Chinatown. Yet one can still see evidence at right that the time-honored custom of posting news and bulletins on certain walls in Chinatown persists.

Two young women attract attention on a rainy Chinatown street, ca. 1918. Although the men may have shorn their queues as directed by the revolutionary spirit of the Chinese Republic, they have not become immune to the novelty of seeing unescorted women on the streets. The man with the street stand on the left may be a fortune-teller.

After 1906, city officials tried their best to relocate Chinatown to the outskirts of the city. Springing into action as officials debated losing Chinatown's tax revenue, a wealthy businessman, Look Tin Eli, developed a plan to rebuild Chinatown in its original location. With a loan from Hong Kong, he commissioned a new commercial building deliberately designed to look "Oriental," and he convinced others to follow his example. This is a view of Grant Avenue (once Dupont Street) facing north, ca. 1918.

By 1925, when this view was taken, Chinese civic and commercial structures had filled in both sides of Stockton Street. This is a view looking north from above Clay Street. The building on the left behind the iron fence is the Chinese Six Companies' headquarters.

Few people can remember a time when there were not matching three-tiered pagoda bookends on Grant Avenue, yet these were modern marvels in their day. The first one to be built, in 1910, is the second building shown here, the Sing Chong Bazaar, built by second-generation businessman Look Tin Eli. On the opposite corner is the Sing Fat Bazaar, built in 1915 by merchant Tong Bong. Both were designed by architects Ross and Bungren and were essentially modern commercial architecture of that era embellished with fanciful Chinese details. They are shown here around 1928.

Historians speculate that this haunting Los Angeles scene entitled "Neighbors of the Alley" was photographed on a Hollywood movie set around 1922. Certainly there was no building with such features ever photographed before in the city's Chinatown. In classic Hollywood style, the re-creation is more beautiful and more mysterious than the original.

Historians may be correct that this photograph entitled "News Travels Fast," showing five Chinese men reading Chinese newspapers posted on a wall, was also taken on a Hollywood movie set. In 1922 the silent movie *The Toll of the Sea* was filmed, starring a beautiful, 15-year-old Anna May Wong, the great Chinese American actress.

The downward spiral of old Chinatown in Los Angeles began about 1910. Thriving businesses moved to a new area, leaving vacant buildings and unpaved streets. Constant litigation and rumors of redevelopment kept the streets unpaved. That was the sinister place depicted in Roman Polanski's 1974 film noir *Chinatown*. This photograph shows Chinese shacks, then probably abandoned, at the rear of South Alameda, at Apaplasa Street. Amid the ruin of old Chinatown, a new Hall of Justice rises in the distance.

Much of old Chinatown in Los Angeles was demolished in the 1920s and 1930s. Authorities investigating an outbreak of pneumonic plague found this Chinese noodle factory still in operation at 414-418 North Alameda, near Aliso Street, ca. 1924.

After years of litigation and fund-raising, the Central Plaza of a new Chinatown in Los Angeles celebrated its grand opening on June 25, 1938. An additional development, shown here from Broadway facing east, was completed one year later, built by You Chung Hong, the first accredited Chinese lawyer in California. Designed by architects Erle Webster and Adrian Wilson, the gate has a four-character poem at top and was originally named the Gate of Maternal Virtue, dedicated to Hong's mother. It is now called the East Gate. Most of old Chinatown had been razed by this time, a portion of it occupied by Union Station. New Chinatown continued to grow in the decades that followed, and at last count had 15,000 residents of mixed nationality.

This was a big step up from delivering vegetables in baskets suspended from poles. By 1915, the successful Chinese American owner of the Chew Hing Company in Oakland, Hing Hon Chew, had this impressive new delivery truck. The driver may be his son, Calvin, who used to ride all over north Oakland and Berkeley, delivering produce to residents. Calvin later opened Grove Supermarket on Grove Street (now Martin Luther King Jr. Way).

Like the Donaldina Cameron House in San Francisco, the Ming Quong Home for Chinese Girls, established in Oakland in 1925, helped orphaned or abandoned girls. Their first facility, designed by Julia Morgan, was traded to nearby Mills College in 1936 in exchange for two other Oakland sites. One, the former Spreckels estate, housed girls from preschool to 13 years, and the other, a facility near Lake Merritt, was later demolished for construction of a BART station. This late-1920s photo was taken at the original Mills College site. The girls are (left to right) Betty Low, Eva Lum, Monica Wong, Eva Chin, Ellen Wu, Genevieve Ki, Mary Fong, Connie Lee, and Dorothy Quan.

Emma Hoo Tom, seen here as a young girl in Oakland, and Clara Chan Lee, wife of pioneering Oakland dentist Dr. Charles Lee, were the first women of any nationality to register to vote in the United States. Emma registered in 1911, when she was 22 years old, after the progressive California state legislature granted women the right to vote in statewide elections. Tom and Lee's history-making activism advanced the rights of women of all races in the United States. Their husbands, who were active in the Native Sons of the Golden State (later called the Chinese American Citizens Alliance), were said to have encouraged the two women to break new ground. They could register to vote because they were born in the United States and thus were citizens.

Along with strictly Chinese holidays like Chinese New Year and Double Ten Day, celebrating the Chinese Republic, San Francisco Chinatown residents also celebrated the birth of the United States, even though its laws continued to discriminate against and segregate the Chinese. Here Richard Mark and Thelma Lee pose before an American flag, ready to light a prodigious string of firecrackers to celebrate Independence Day 1934.

The heart of new Chinatown, Grant Avenue at Sacramento Street, is shown here around 1930. At left in the foreground is the W. Sang Lung Company Bazaar, and to the right in the foreground is the Canton Bazaar, which is still in business today at 616 Grant Avenue.

The playground of the first kindergarten in San Francisco's Chinatown is shown here on September 7, 1934. According to teacher and author Dr. Judy Yung, the kindergarten was a product of Franklin Roosevelt's New Deal. It operated in the Chinese YWCA on Joice Street on land provided by the Chinese Presbyterian Church. It can be noted that all of the teachers are Caucasian in this photo.

The children in this 1934 image seem ready to hang lanterns. The lantern at the bottom reads "longevity," and so they may be honoring an elder's birthday. Identified from top to bottom are Gilbert Dere, Janet Jean, Shirley Poo, Gwendolyn Chan, and Delores Poo.

The signs in this 1935 view of Grant Avenue from Pine Street are now in both Chinese and English. This is evidence of Chinatown's focus on tourism and the increased presence by then of second-generation Chinese Americans who read and spoke English as a first language.

The women shown in February 1936 in this basement "sweatshop" are two of about two hundred National Dollar Store garment workers in Chinatown who organized a Chinese Ladies' Garment Workers Union, Local 341. Although National Dollar Store, founded and owned by Chinese immigrant Joe Shoong, was the largest employer in Chinatown, there were about 1,000 female garment workers in Chinatown. Local 341 led a successful strike in 1938 to increase wages at National, but soon after their groundbreaking victory, the company was sold and the new company shut down the factory, and all of the National Dollar Store workers lost their jobs.

It is believed that the kite was invented in China over 2,000 years ago. One version of the history credits Mo Di, a philosopher who lived on Mount Lu. The first recorded kites were used for military purposes, including kites large enough to carry a man over enemy walls as a spy. Kites spread to the common folk in China during the Tang dynasty (618–907 A.D.) and spread throughout Europe and the New World. The Chinese have a special love of the kite, known as *fengzheng*. These two young ladies were the kite-flying champions of Chinatown on March 2, 1936.

During the early years of the gold rush, there was so little fresh water and so few women in San Francisco that it was cheaper to buy new shirts than have them laundered. Chinese immigrants filled this need by picking up and delivering the laundry of desperate '49ers. All they needed was a source of water, a flatiron, and baskets. Later they opened laundry businesses and have dominated the laundry trade in San Francisco ever since. This venerable service has evolved its own traditions. Pictured here is a San Francisco laundry in 1937. The man in the background is brush-painting customers' identification marks in Chinese characters, including, "Smiling lady with big bosom," "Man who squints," and "Lady with many husbands."

The San Francisco–Oakland Bay Bridge has been called the ugly stepsister of the famed Golden Gate Bridge, which has always been favored by the world at large. Yet to residents of the two cities, the opening of the Bay Bridge on November 12, 1936, was a momentous occasion, linking two sister cities and two Chinatowns with many family ties. Four times as long and twice as busy as the Golden Gate, the Bay Bridge was feted with much ceremony, celebration, and a large parade, including this beautiful pagoda float, and (not shown) a huge Golden Dragon and marching units.

June and Doris Wong play beside an outsized mask stuck in the sands of Treasure Island on November 10, 1937. The mask is destined to ornament the 1939 Golden Gate International Exposition, but first it will be a "Halloween frightener" at a benefit bazaar sponsored by the Paulist Fathers Catholic Mission in October 1937.

The buildup to the Golden Gate International Exposition began in 1933. This basket maker, photographed in April 1938, would demonstrate Chinese basket-making at the fair, planned to celebrate the opening of the San Francisco–Oakland Bay Bridge and the Golden Gate Bridge in 1936 and 1937 respectively. The exposition site, Treasure Island, was an artificial plot of land built by the federal government where the two spans of the Bay Bridge met. It was planned to serve as an airport, but was instead taken over by the U.S. Navy during World War II.

The Golden Gate International Exposition ran from February 18 through October 29, 1939, and again from May 25 through September 29, 1940. The theme for the fair was Gateway to the Pacific. Shown here is the entrance to the Chinese Village on the "Gayway." The Gayway was the fun center of the island, where visitors were offered every type of entertainment from "weird" Chinese music, as it was described, to roller coaster rides.

Chinese actors are in full theatrical costume to be part of an international parade at the Golden Gate International Exposition on Treasure Island. Seen here on July 3, 1939, at the entrance to the Chinese Village, the actors also wore these elaborate costumes for stage performances at the village theater.

Although they no longer dominated California agriculture by the mid–twentieth century, some Chinese still tilled the good earth. In this photo an unidentified Chinese orchardist tends his vegetable garden in Placer County in December 1940.

Captain James Der of the Chinese Junior Traffic Patrol directs a group of students at a busy Chinatown street corner on April 18, 1938. To avoid the many traffic accidents involving schoolchildren on congested streets, a Junior Traffic Patrol was established. Boys and girls crossing Stockton and Clay streets had extra protection from that time on.

Shown here May 1, 1941, is a typical afternoon at Washington and Stockton streets as school lets out for lunch. These traffic patrol boys did triple duty, since the regular parochial school conducted at the Catholic Chinese Mission ran from 9:00 A.M. to 3:10 P.M., and two other nearby schools were operated from 4:00 to 6:00, and from 5:00 P.M. to 8:00 P.M. In the three years since the patrol had been established, no child had been killed at a crossing.

Even before the United States entered World War II, the citizens of Chinatown were busy raising money to aid Chinese refugees displaced by Japanese aggression. This "Rice Bowl" celebration at the Chinese music pavilion on Grant Avenue on May 3, 1941, brought in more donations. Either the Cathayans or the Chinatown Knights may have been on the program that night, as both orchestras played music for this cause.

Representatives of the Chinese Six Companies, formed in the 1850s and acting representative of the Chinese in the United States, await the arrival of Madame Chiang Kai-shek, charismatic wife of Chinese leader Chiang Kai-shek, on March 20, 1943. Madame Chiang toured the West to raise awareness and money for the war with Japan. Later, Chiang Kai-shek's Kuomintang Nationalist government would battle the Communists before being exiled to Taiwan in 1949. At this time the Chinese Six Companies were entirely sympathetic with Madame Chiang Kai-shek's cause.

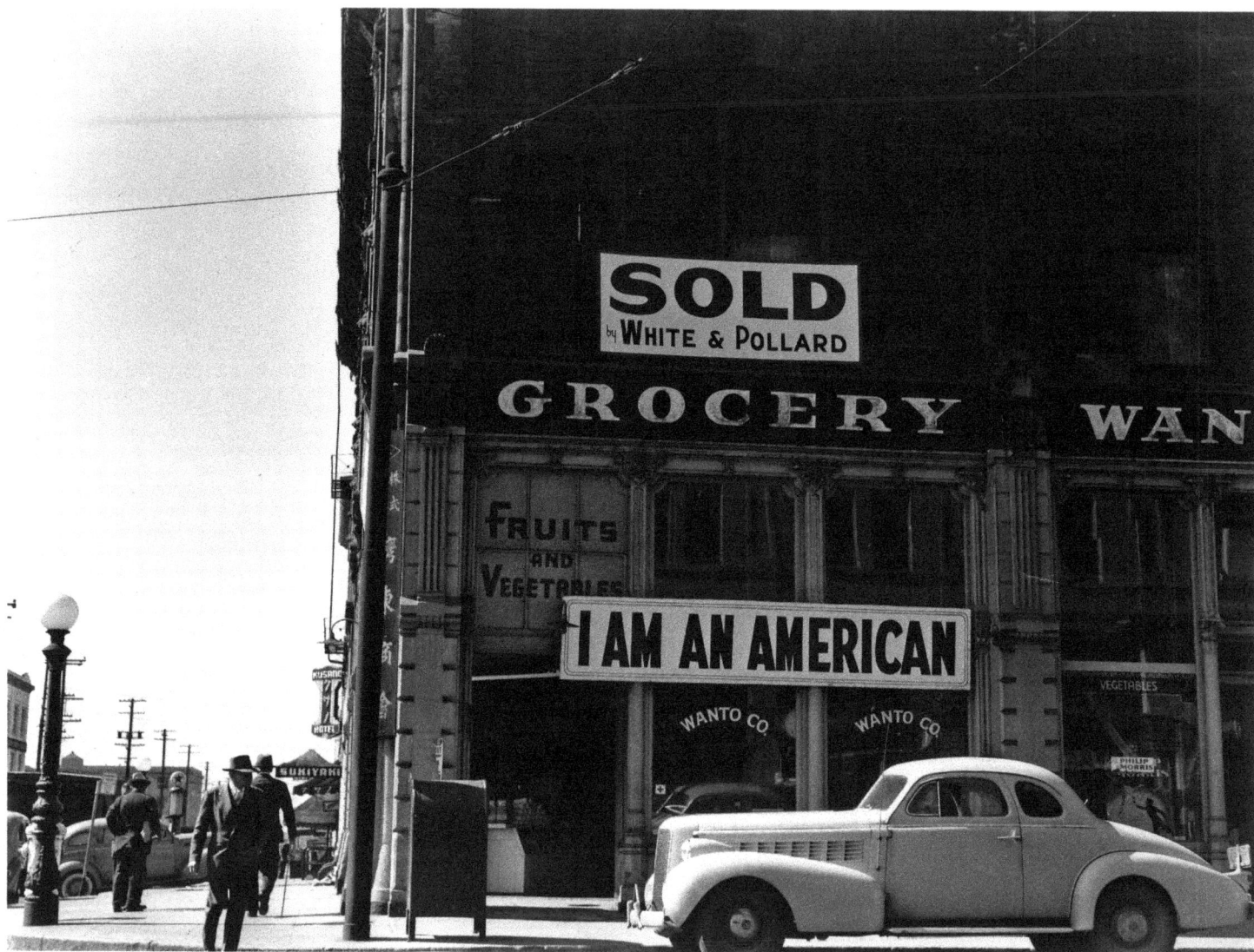

An unidentified Japanese American owned this Oakland grocery store at 401 Eighth Street, at Franklin Street, at the time of the attack on Pearl Harbor, December 7, 1941. He told photographer Dorothea Lange, who took this photograph in early 1942, that he purchased the banner to make his position clear the day after the attack. It did little good. A few months later, he joined other West Coast Japanese Americans evacuated to remote internment camps. Four Chinese families purchased this store. After 1900, Japanese immigrants had begun to replace Chinese agricultural workers. In 1942 the trend was reversed: many Japanese-owned farms and businesses were purchased by Chinese Americans.

When Japanese families were interned in 1942, the California Farm Bureau estimated they raised nearly 40 percent of the state's fruits and vegetables. The editor of the *Chinese Press,* Charles Leong, said, "Chinese remember that their parents labored on farms in the Sacramento and San Joaquin valleys and all along coastal farm areas . . . But . . . the ranch life, a hard life, did not appeal to the second generation." This photograph shows a member of the Negi family completing negotiations with a Chinese businessman to take over the family's leased 40-acre truck farm in Hayward (now Hesperian Boulevard) at the time of their "voluntary evacuation to Colorado," as described in the photo record.

For decades, Chinese men would gather at certain walls in San Francisco's Chinatown to read the news and bulletins posted there. The first Chinese newspaper in the United States was the short-lived *Golden Hills News*. The most famous and lasting of the Chinese language newspapers was *Chung Sai Yat Po,* published in San Francisco from 1900 to 1951. Owned and edited by devout Christians, it recorded the history of the Chinese in San Francisco over those decades. Here men inspect the edition for March 8, 1944, no doubt carrying news of the war. The Chinese letters at top may be translated as "Gold Mountain Daily Newspaper," and by this time the term Gold Mountain referred to San Francisco, not the entire state.

Chinese Americans were not treated as equals in the United States armed forces in the early 1900s. To rectify this, Chinatown's American Legion Cathay Post, No. 384, was established on August 24, 1931. Thousands of Chinese Americans and immigrants answered the call to defend the United States during World War II, and hundreds were killed in action. After the war, veterans were allowed to become naturalized citizens, take advantage of the GI Bill, and bring their wives and children from China to America. Here the Cathay Post is seen around 1944, when it had almost 1,500 members.

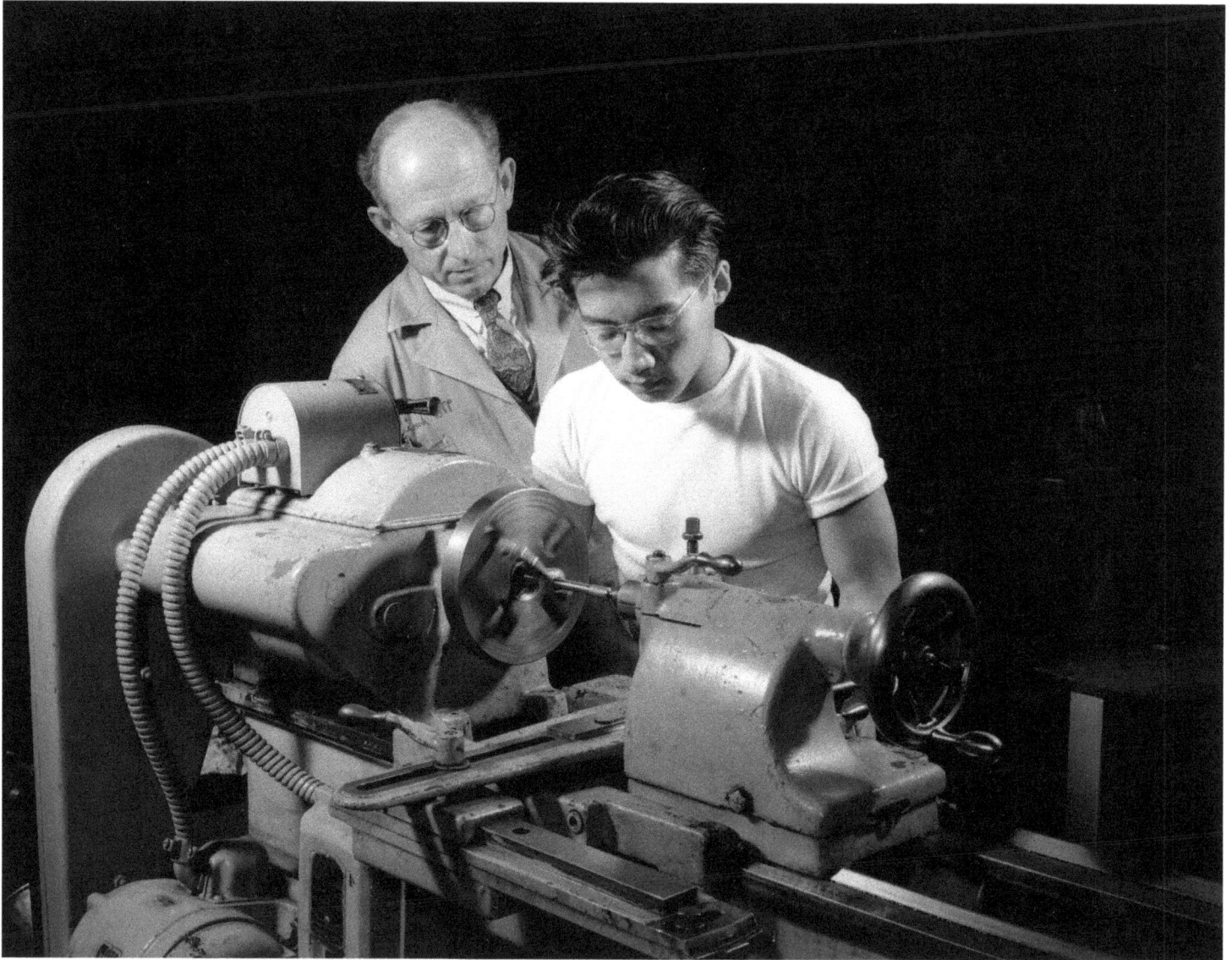

Conditions improved for the Chinese in Los Angeles after World War II, as in every part of California. Chinese children began to be admitted to California's public schools in the 1920s, and by 1942, the schools were fully integrated. This Chinese student is part of the High School Victory Corps at Los Angeles Polytechnic High School, helping with the war effort by learning to operate a lathe.

The Chinatown YWCA was founded in San Francisco in 1916. In 1932, the YWCA moved into a lovely building designed by noted architect Julia Morgan at 965 Clay Street. In this photograph, a YWCA member strikes a bell while entertaining servicemen on May 25, 1945. Currently, the old YWCA building houses the Chinese Historical Society of America, established in 1963 with the mission to educate and foster the understanding of the Chinese experience in America.

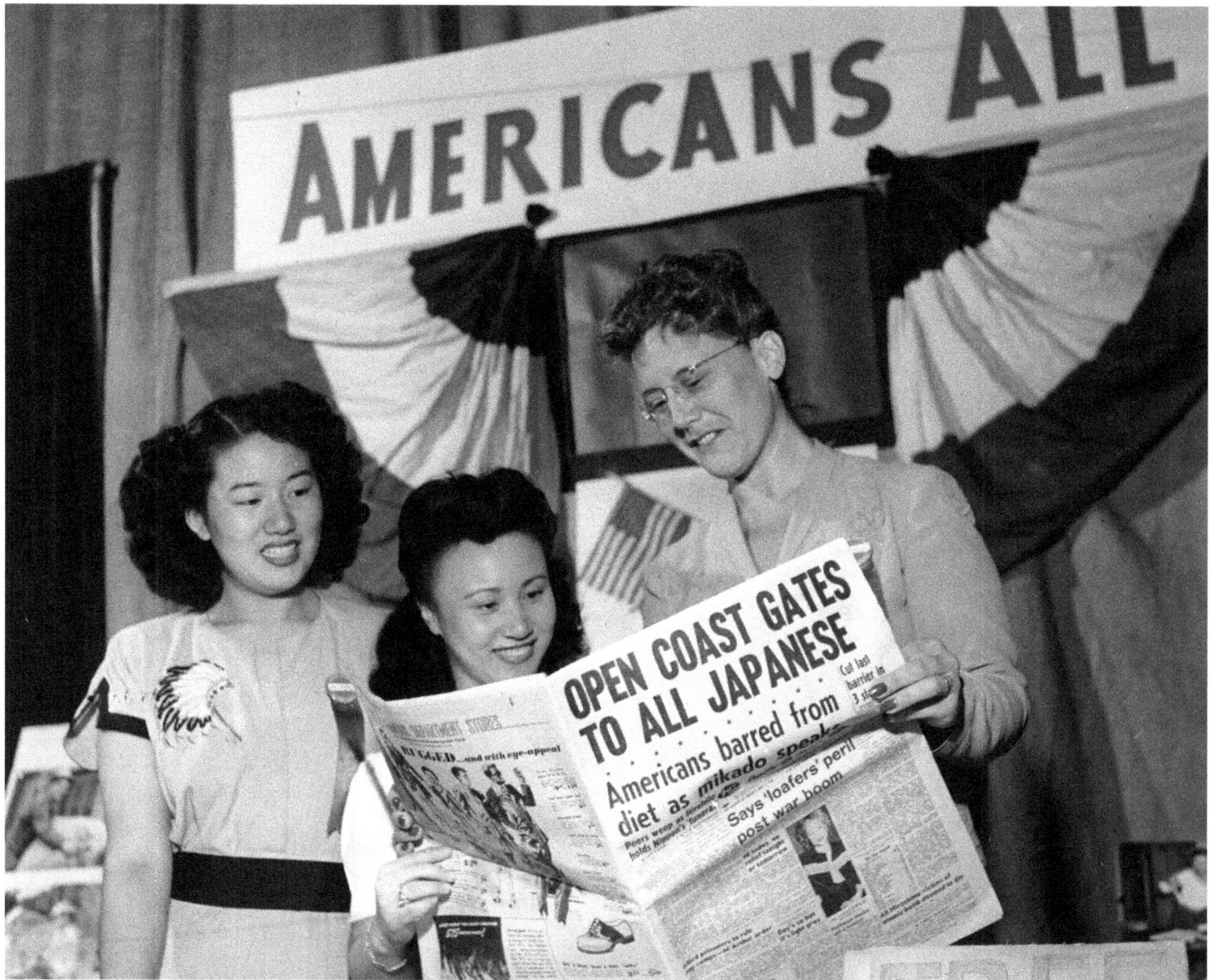

The "Americans All" booth at the Pan-Pacific Industrial Exposition in Los Angeles was sponsored by groups opposed to racial discrimination, in cooperation with the War Relocation Authority (WRA), the agency given oversight of the Japanese internment camps during World War II. Featured at the booth was a continuous motion picture showing of *Nisei in Action* and *World We Want to Live In.* Working and standing together on September 6, 1945, are (right to left) Mrs. Sylvia Leventhal of B'nai B'rith Women, Los Angeles; Miss Eva Lee, an American of Chinese descent of the International Institute in Los Angeles; and Miss Mary Suzuki of the WRA Area Office in Los Angeles (formerly of Manzanar, a Japanese internment camp).

The Bowen/Wing family, gathered at Grayce Bowen Wye's Oakland home at 564 Sixty-second Street, is dressed like any middle-class family in Oakland at the time. From left to right are (front row) Rally Eng, Rhetta Wing Ah-Tye, and Wendell Wye; (second row) John Won; (third row) Joyce Wye Mar, Mary Bowen Wing, Elyse Bowen Won, Janie Wing Dang; (top row) Grayce Bowen Wye, Florence Bowen Eng, and Pauline Wing Lou.

A produce truck belonging to Henry Lum is seen here in the early 1940s. Lum was born in China and came to California intent on making enough money to pay off his father's gambling debts. After working on a dude ranch and as a "house boy," he went back to China, married, and returned with his wife and son to Nevada. Eventually settling in Oakland, they opened a mom-and-pop grocery store and delivered fresh produce to the Oakland and Berkeley hills. Pictured from left to right are Ruby Lum, May Lum, Peggy Lum, and Chan Lin Lum, mother of the three girls and wife of Henry.

A California Street cable car passes by in this view down Grant Avenue in 1945. Where the old Sing Chong Bazaar once operated, at left, a sign on the building reads "Cathay House," advertising a Chinese restaurant still in operation today.

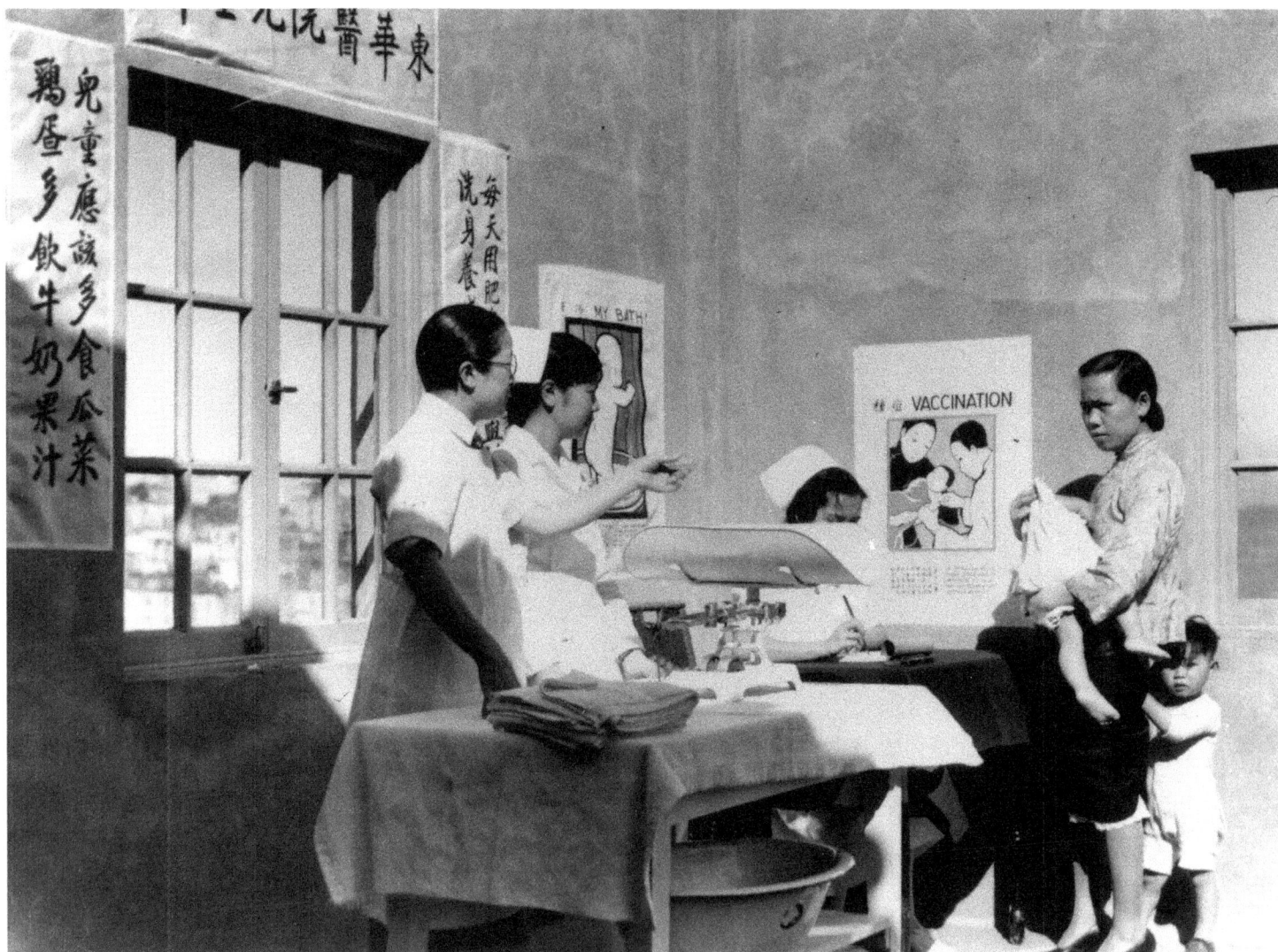

The segregated Chinese population was not admitted to San Francisco hospitals. For many years the only medical facility available was the Tung Wah Dispensary, staffed by missionaries. In 1925, 15 Chinese service organizations came together to build the first and only Chinese hospital in the United States, on Jackson Street. Pictured here around 1945, it continues to operate today. The banner at top reads: "Dong Hwa Hospital." The sign on the left says: "Children should eat more vegetables and eggs and drink more milk and juice."

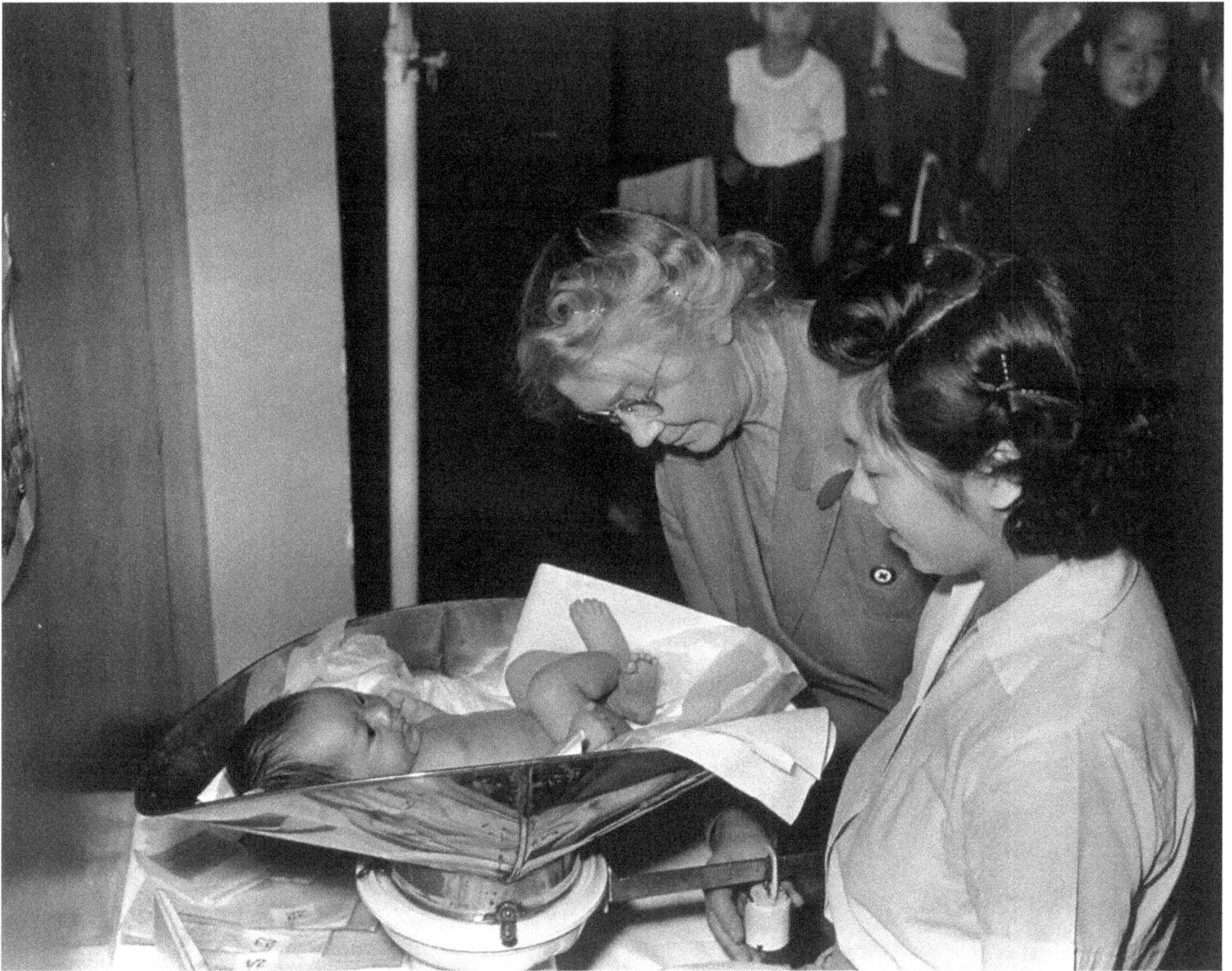

A new infant is weighed at the Chinese hospital on Jackson Street, ca. 1944. Although it represented a great improvement to Chinese health care when it was built in 1925, the hospital could not prevent overcrowding and poverty in Chinatown, where tuberculosis killed three times as many people as it did in other San Francisco neighborhoods in the 1940s.

These Chinese children are marching down Grant Avenue during the annual celebration of Double Ten Day to commemorate the founding of the Chinese Republic on October 10, 1911. American and Chinese flags fly on October 11, 1945, as they pass the old Sing Fat Bazaar and Sing Chong Bazaar buildings on California Street.

Miss Ruby Fong teaches Chinese reading and writing to second grade students at St. Mary's Chinese School on June 15, 1945. The children attended classes at St. Mary's, operated by the Paulist Fathers, in the afternoon, following public school classes. Attendance was voluntary, but about 400 students were enrolled. A rough translation of the words the children are writing would read: "There is boundless happiness in learning/reading." In other words, learning is fun.

A group of Chinese technicians, awaiting departure for China, have gathered in Civic Center Plaza on July 10, 1946. Shown are a small number of the 1,100 Chinese men enrolled in the Training Programs for Chinese Technicians, sponsored by the Chinese Supply Commission of the Republic of China. They will return to their county aboard the SS *General Gordon*. At right stands one of the three Civic Center dormitories built to accommodate the technicians while they prepared to leave.

This aerial view of Chinatown was taken March 7, 1947, to illustrate a newspaper article in the *San Francisco Call Bulletin* about overcrowding. In 1947 about 17,000 adults and 6,000 children lived in a 20-block area of Chinatown. The paper noted that "vaccine may be used in Chinatown to reduce the murderous TB rate."

This was one of several photos used by District Attorney Pat Brown as evidence of the crowded conditions in San Francisco's Chinatown tenements as he indicted unsatisfactory living conditions as a major cause of crime and disease in San Francisco. It is dated May 7, 1947. He described this as a "typical Chinatown apartment," with eight people living in two rooms. The old law prohibiting Chinese from owning property outside of Chinatown, essentially segregating them into a ghetto, was finally repealed in 1948. District Attorney Pat Brown later became governor of California.

Six thousand Chinatown children had only this half-acre playground for recreation in February 1948. The playground was built in 1927 on Sacramento Street between Hang Ah Alley and Waverly Place. The Chinese Public Affairs Committee asked for a modern recreation center with a plunge, gymnasium, hobby rooms, and rooftop playground. The clubhouse is shown at right, and farther to the right, not pictured here, was a basketball court. When this playground was rebuilt in the 1980s, it was renamed Willie Woo Woo Wong Playground after a prominent Chinese American basketball player.

Soon after Chinese veterans of World War II were given the opportunity to retrieve their wives and minor children in China through the War Brides and Chinese Alien Wives Acts in December 1945, many pretty new faces appeared in Chinatown. Mrs. James Lee of the YWCA is shown here teaching the war brides English on February 29, 1948. She also taught them about American government, and helped them write letters home to China, urging their homeland to combat the spread of Communism. According to teacher and author Dr. Judy Yung, almost 6,000 Chinese women immigrated to the United States after Congress passed these acts.

The Yerba Buena block was demolished in March 1950 to make room for the Ping Yuen Housing Development. Heralded in publicity as the "first good housing ever to be built in Chinatown," it rose where older buildings, some that had withstood the earthquake, fell. The plan, according to the newspaper account, was for modern, pleasant apartments with a Chinese motif and plenty of garden and play space for 234 low-income families.

By September 27, 1951, the new Ping Yuen (Tranquil Gardens) apartments were rapidly approaching completion on Pacific Avenue between Columbus Avenue and Stockton Street. The project represented new Chinatown, where "modern, airy apartments will be available . . . to Chinese who have lived in crowded rooms and narrow alleys for generations." Managers received 600 applications for 234 apartments of one to three bedrooms, renting for $15 to $60 per month, depending upon the applicant's income. After clamoring for low-cost public housing for 12 years, the community finally had three six-story apartment buildings.

With visions of airy, modern apartments probably dancing in his head, one reporter saw narrow back alleys, like Spofford Alley, shown here September 27, 1951, where "the family wash hangs out over the narrow street," as a thing of the past. No longer forced to remain within the 20 blocks of Chinatown, an Asian exodus began, first to the Richmond and Sunset districts, and then to every neighborhood in the Bay Area and state. Mostly the elderly and poor were left behind.

These twin lions danced through the streets of Chinatown on January 31, 1952, hoping to collect donations for the Chinese hospital. Merchants hung strings of money from the awnings of their shops to feed the hungry lions, and firecrackers were thrown at their feet. Following behind in a truck were Chinese musicians, perhaps the Cathay Boys Band. In 1951, a similar event had collected $9,000.

Traffic congestion in tourist-choked Chinatown was a major problem for pedestrians. This young man points out a new traffic sign to ladies who may be endangered by stepping out on this street on September 25, 1953. The sign states, "Pedestrians may not cross the street from this point." It was located at 1201 Grant Avenue, at Broadway.

A resurgence of crime on the streets of Chinatown may have necessitated the return of uniformed officers walking a regular Chinatown beat starting August 8, 1955. There had been no regular patrol assigned to the 20-block area since 1880. Here Edward Nevin (left) and James B. Dowd, both members of the former plainclothes "Chinatown Squad," patrol Pelton Place.

Despite a concerted crackdown in the 1920s on the Chinatown tongs that controlled gambling and other illicit activities, gambling apparently still flourished in Chinatown in the 1950s. This raid on a parlor at 1034 Stockton Street on April 7, 1955, indicates that famed Chinatown Squad chief Jack Manion may have overestimated his achievements in cleaning out the highbinders. In the foreground at left, the district attorney's investigator A. L. Lamport talks to Huie Lai, who was later arrested as a dealer.

This Double Ten Day celebration on October 10, 1955, had an additional weapon to fight the cold war. The venerable Golden Dragon was equipped with electric lights in order to help ward off Communism in the Free World. An annual event sponsored by the Chinese Six Companies to celebrate the founding of the Chinese Republic in 1911, this year the event was cosponsored by the Anti-Communist League.

The Hoy Fung Cantonese Opera Club, seen performing February 2, 1960, brought the musical heritage of old Guangdong Province to San Franciscans. But the orchestra was involved in more than just music. During World War II, the club provided daily meals to members. In 1961 it raised funds for famine relief in China.

Chinese-run businesses had to do without an answering service until 1962, when Ben and Nora Wong opened the first Chinese answering service in the West. Like the operators at the earlier Chinese telephone exchange, these operators had to be fluent in several Cantonese and Mandarin dialects. It was a sign of the times, however, that the service also employed someone who spoke Italian and Spanish. Seen here at the switchboard is Nora Long (left) and the couple's daughter, Gloria Wong.

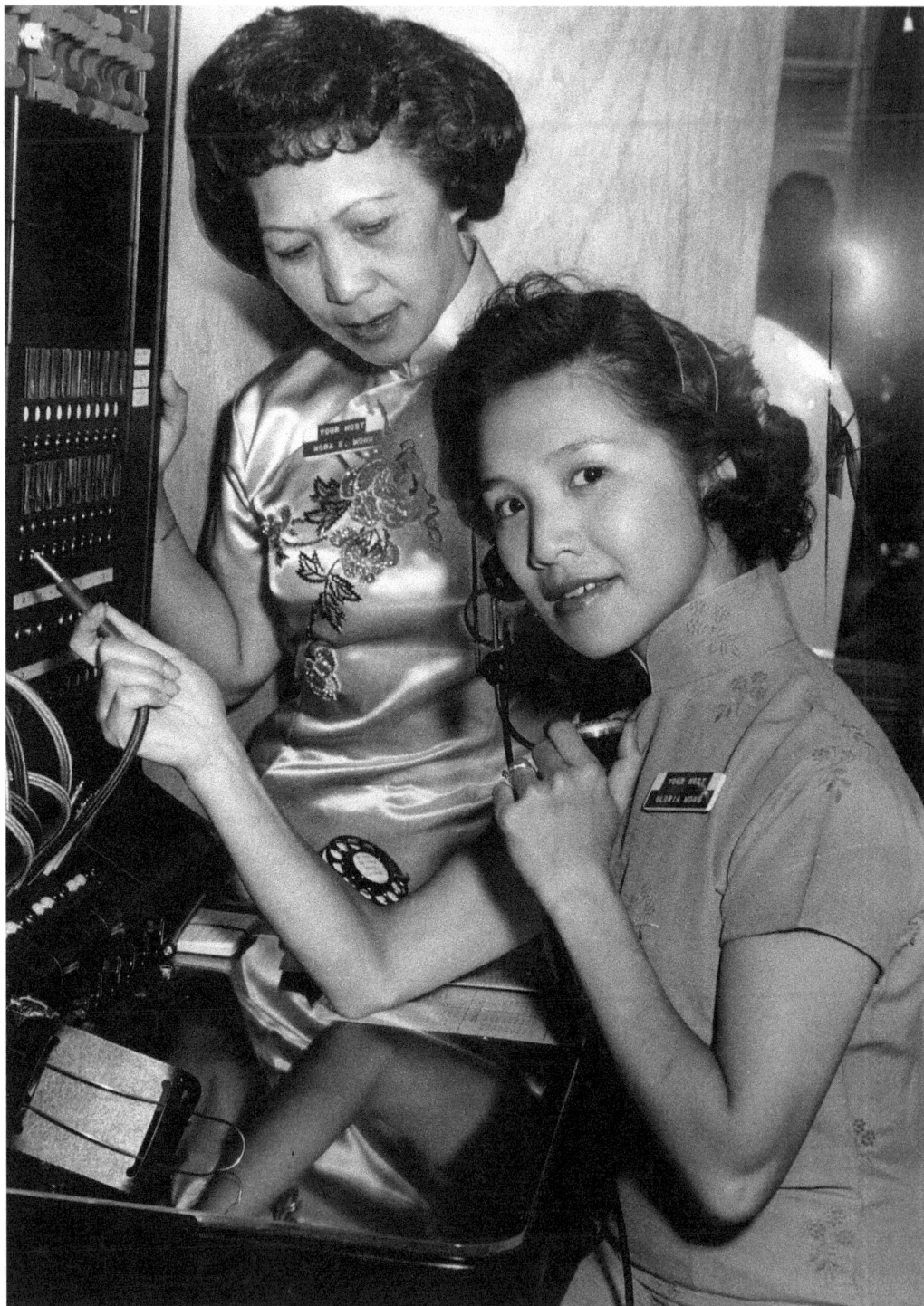

Many merchants carried herbal medicines in early Chinatown, but the first Chinese-owned pharmacy was Man Quong Fong's Republic Drug Company, opened on Grant Avenue in November 1912. Some of the early San Francisco Chinese physicians were Margaret Chung, James H. Hall, Rose G. Wong, and C. Y. Low. By the time this photograph of Republic Drug Company pharmacist Lela Dong was taken, February 12, 1959, there were 40 physicians and 8 pharmacies serving San Francisco's Chinese community.

Since its inception in 1958, the Miss Chinatown USA contest has given young Chinese women from across the country the opportunity to win scholarships and become goodwill ambassadors for the Chinese community. They are judged on talent, grace, and intellect. In 1961 Irene Tsu (second from left) took away top honors. She and the runners-up hopped a ride on the California Street cable car on the way to a celebratory breakfast at the Mark Hopkins Hotel.

The St. Mary's Chinese Girls Drum Corps march in the Double Ten Day Parade in 1964. No longer hidden away in their Chinatown homes, young Chinese women in San Francisco were now an integral part of the public events and entertainments in San Francisco.

Glitter and glamour drew tourists to Chinatown nightlife in the 1950s and 1960s. No longer a segregated neighborhood, Chinatown made the most of its restaurants and nightclubs featuring Chinese musicians and entertainers. This scene was captured around 1958.

Since they began arriving on the shores of California, Chinese immigrants disproved the American "melting pot" myth. Segregation and discrimination as well as strong ties to their homeland kept them in a world apart in San Francisco. Yet that segregation had one unintended benefit: keeping Chinese culture and traditions alive for a new generation of Chinese Americans in California. Wesley Wong and Cynthia Jung peek out from the mouth of a lion, February 18, 1964.

Notes on the Photographs

These notes, listed by page number, attempt to include all aspects known of the photographs. Each of the photographs is identified by the page number, a title or description, photographer and collection, archive, and call or box number when applicable. Although every attempt was made to collect all data, in some cases complete data may have been unavailable due to the age and condition of some of the photographs and records.

114 **MAN FUNG WO STORE**
San Francisco History
Center, San Francisco Public
Library
AAB-7129

115 **YOUNGSTERS IN
PORTSMOUTH SQUARE**
Courtesy of The Bancroft
Library
University of California,
Berkeley
I0012674

116 **ANGEL ISLAND
IMMIGRATION STATION
COURTESY OF THE
BANCROFT LIBRARY**
University of California,
Berkeley
brk00001186_16a

117 **ANGEL ISLAND
EXAMINATION ROOM**
Courtesy of The Bancroft
Library
University of California,
Berkeley
brk00001192_16a

118 **ANGEL ISLAND
KITCHEN**
Courtesy of The Bancroft
Library
University of California,
Berkeley
brk00001194_16a

119 **SUN LOUIE SUN HONG**
Courtesy of The Bancroft
Library
University of California,
Berkeley
brk00001305_16a

120 **CATHAY CHINESE BOYS
BAND**
San Francisco History
Center, San Francisco Public
Library
AAB-6860

121 **CHINATOWN KNIGHTS**
San Francisco History
Center, San Francisco Public
Library
AAB-7018

122 **CHINESE NEW YEAR'S
PARADE**
Courtesy of The Bancroft
Library
University of California,
Berkeley
brk00001312_16a

123 **GROUND-BREAKING
CEREMONY**
San Francisco History
Center, San Francisco Public
Library
AAB-0383

124 **CHINESE MUSICAL
THEATER**
San Francisco History
Center, San Francisco Public
Library
AAB-7274

125 **LOUIS WANG**
Photo by Mervyn Silberstein;
Courtesy of Gloria S. Brown

126 **FIREWORKS IN
CHINATOWN**
Photo by Mervyn Silberstein;
Courtesy of Gloria S. Brown

127 **BOY ON TRICYCLE**
Photo by Mervyn Silberstein;
Courtesy of Gloria S. Brown

128 **BALLOON VENDOR**
Photo by Mervyn Silberstein;
Courtesy of Gloria S. Brown

129 **MAN ROASTING
CHESTNUTS**
Photo by Mervyn Silberstein;
Courtesy of Gloria S. Brown

130 **CHINESE BOYS ON
COBBLED STREET**
Photo by Mervyn Silberstein;
Courtesy of Gloria S. Brown

131 **SIDEWALK VENDOR**
Photo by Mervyn Silberstein;
Courtesy of Gloria S. Brown

132 **WOMAN AND HER INFANT**
Photo by Mervyn Silberstein;
Courtesy of Gloria S. Brown

133 **PATRIARCH AND FAMILY**
Photo by Mervyn Silberstein;
Courtesy of Gloria S. Brown

134 **WOMAN ON BALCONY**
Photo by Mervyn Silberstein;
Courtesy of Gloria S. Brown

135 **ROSS ALLEY**
Photo by Mervyn Silberstein;
Courtesy of Gloria S. Brown

136 **TWO YOUNG WOMEN ON A
CORNER**
Courtesy of The Bancroft
Library
University of California,
Berkeley
I0012657

137 **GRANT AVENUE**
San Francisco History
Center, San Francisco Public
Library
AAB-6814

138 **STOCKTON STREET**
Courtesy of The Bancroft
Library
University of California,
Berkeley
I0050690

139 **SING CHONG BAZAAR**
Library of Congress
LC-USZ62-98492-
3b44570u

140 **NEIGHBORS OF THE
ALLEY**
Photo by Paul Grenbeaux;
Library of Congress
LC-USZ62-108269-
3c08269u

141 **NEWS TRAVELS FAST**
Photo by Paul Grenbeaux;
Library of Congress
LC-USZ62-109112

142 **LOS ANGELES
CHINATOWN SHACKS**
Courtesy of The Bancroft
Library
University of California,
Berkeley
I0027637

143 **LOS ANGELES NOODLE
FACTORY**
Courtesy of The Bancroft
Library
University of California,
Berkeley
I0027606

HISTORIC PHOTOS OF THE CHINESE IN CALIFORNIA

The Chinese were a visible current in the tidal wave of humanity that rushed through San Francisco's Golden Gate in the mid–nineteenth century. Known to their countrymen as Gam Saan Haak (guests of Gold Mountain), Chinese immigrants sought great fortune. Most found only hostility and hard work, often braving the most dangerous and loathsome jobs. They endured violence and injustice, yet clung to this land with tenacity and patience and made it their own.

With nearly 200 historic photographs gathered from notable collections, this book explores a century of Chinese progress in California. Retracing the immigrants' steps—from the gold fields to the high Sierra railroad camps, to lettuce fields and olive groves, and the Monterey coast—we visit Chinese enclaves throughout the state. We linger in San Francisco's old Chinatown, home to cherished children and notorious tong gangs, where new arrivals first found refuge and aging storefronts offered exotic merchandise and leaked pungent odors. These historic images recall a time when the Chinese community in California was still a world apart.

Hannah Clayborn was born and raised in Oakland. A professional historian, writer, and editor, she has lived in the San Francisco Bay Area her entire life. Earning undergraduate degrees in anthropology and psychology and a graduate degree in history, she went on to serve as the director of four history museums in the Greater Bay Area. Her early investigations into the history of Chinese and other immigrant groups in two rural communities in Northern California led to several articles. She has published historical books and articles on the towns of Bloomfield and Healdsburg, and has edited more than 100 pictorial histories of California cities and towns. She is currently editing a new history of Walnut Creek, California, where she lives with her husband and two daughters.

WWW.TURNERPUBLISHING.COM